FIONA BRIMBLECOMBE

DEFAMATION IN THE DIGITAL AGE AND THE 'RIGHT TO BE FORGOTTEN'

First published in Great Britain in 2025 by

Bristol University Press
University of Bristol
1–9 Old Park Hill
Bristol
BS2 8BB
UK
t: +44 (0)117 374 6645
e: bup-info@bristol.ac.uk

Details of international sales and distribution partners are available at bristoluniversitypress.co.uk

© Fiona Brimblecombe 2025

The digital PDF and ePub versions of this title are available open access and distributed under the terms of the Creative Commons Attribution-NonCommercial-NoDerivatives 4.0 International licence (https://creativecommons.org/licenses/by-nc-nd/4.0/) which permits reproduction and distribution for non-commercial use without further permission provided the original work is attributed.

DOI: 10.51952/9781529243024

British Library Cataloguing in Publication Data
A catalogue record for this book is available from the British Library

ISBN 978-1-5292-4300-0 paperback
ISBN 978-1-5292-4301-7 ePub
ISBN 978-1-5292-4302-4 OA PDF

The right of Fiona Brimblecombe to be identified as author of this work has been asserted by her in accordance with the Copyright, Designs and Patents Act 1988.

All rights reserved: no part of this publication may be reproduced, stored in a retrieval system, or transmitted in any form or by any means, electronic, mechanical, photocopying, recording, or otherwise without the prior permission of Bristol University Press.

Every reasonable effort has been made to obtain permission to reproduce copyrighted material. If, however, anyone knows of an oversight, please contact the publisher.

The statements and opinions contained within this publication are solely those of the author and not of the University of Bristol or Bristol University Press. The University of Bristol and Bristol University Press disclaim responsibility for any injury to persons or property resulting from any material published in this publication.

Bristol University Press works to counter discrimination on grounds of gender, race, disability, age and sexuality.

Cover design: blu inc
Front cover image: Alamy/Daniel Krasoń
Bristol University Press uses environmentally responsible print partners.
Printed and bound in Great Britain by CPI Group (UK) Ltd,
Croydon, CR0 4YY

Bristol University Press' authorised representative in the
European Union is: Easy Access System Europe,
Mustamäe tee 50, 10621 Tallinn, Estonia,
Email: gpsr.requests@easproject.com

For my grandfather, William

Contents

Acknowledgements ix

Introduction 1

one Digital Advancements and Threats to Reputation 5
    Introduction 5
    I.   Technological advancements and threats 7
        to reputation
        a. A beginning: the rise of cloud computing 7
           i. Cloud computing and threats 9
             to reputation
        b. The birth of social media 11
           ii. Social media and threats 13
             to reputation
        c. Wide availability of technology 15
           iii. Affordable technology and threats 18
             to reputation
        d. The 'Metaverse' and online worlds 21
           iv. Online worlds and threats 24
             to reputation
        e. Augmented reality 26
           v. Augmented reality and threats 27
             to reputation
        f. Artificial intelligence 28
           vi. Artificial intelligence and threats 31
             to reputation
    Conclusion for Chapter 1 33

two Searching for a Theoretical Basis of 36
    Defamation Law
    Introduction 36

	Part I: The theory		38
	I.	'Dignity' as justifying defamation law	39
		a. The history of dignity	39
		b. Conceptualizing dignity	40
		c. Issues with dignity	42
		i. Definitional difficulties	42
		ii. Dignity and balancing rights	44
		d. 'Rival' theories to reputation as dignity	46
		i. Defamation law as protecting honour	46
		ii. Personality rights as property	48
	II.	The looking-glass self theory	50
	III.	Defamation law as protecting human sociality and relationships	53
		a. Strong and weak ties	57
	IV.	Concluding remarks for Part I	58
	Part II: The scenarios		60
	I.	The *defamation by social media* scenario	60
	II.	The *third-party poster* scenario	61
	III.	The *defamation by AI tool or virtual world* scenario	62
	IV.	The *repetition of statements online over a year later* scenario	63
	V.	Concluding remarks for Part II	64
three	**How Online Defamation Cases Are Decided**		65
	Part I: Difficulties for claimants posed by the Defamation Act 2013		66
	I.	Online publication and the 'serious harm' threshold	67
		a. Background to the reform	67

	b. Interpretive difficulties: what exactly is the new s 1 'serious harm' threshold?	70
	c. How does one evidence serious harm caused or likely to be caused by an online post?	75
	d. What is the significance of viewership and engagement metrics to s 1?	79
	e. Is there a different approach to s 1 where the internet is concerned?	83
	f. Section 1's introduction in the context of the codified defences in the 2013 Act	86
II.	Concluding remarks about s 1 and online defamation	92
III.	The introduction of the single publication rule in s 8 Defamation Act 2013	94
	a. Background to s 8	94
	b. Thin justifications	98
	c. What is republication in 'substantially the same' form?	101
	d. A mitigating factor: s 32A of the Limitation Act 1980	103
IV.	Concluding remarks for Part I	105
Part II: Liability of host websites and defamation by an AI tool		106
I.	The defence for operators of websites under s 5 Defamation Act 2013	107
	a. A new defence	107
	b. Potential issues	110
	c. Approach of the Strasbourg Court	112
II.	Defamation by an AI tool	120
	a. A rising threat	120
	b. The nature of the threat	123
	c. Who should be responsible for an AI tool's defamatory speech?	125

		d. Deepfakes and defamation	131
	III.	Concluding remarks for Part II	136
	Conclusion for Chapter 3		137

four **Routes to Remedy? The 'Right to Be Forgotten' as an Alternative Route to Redress** — 139

Introduction — 139
Part I: What is the right to be forgotten? — 141
    I.   Background context — 141
    II. Article 17 GDPR — 145
Part II: Can the 'right to be forgotten' provide a more effective remedy than English defamation law? — 149
    I.   Accessibility of redress — 149
    II. Hurdles to making a claim — 153
    III. Decision making — 160
    IV. *Ex post* remedies — 167
    V. The 'right to be forgotten' and the *data-dissemination* scenarios — 168
    VI. Future of the 'right to be forgotten' in UK and European law — 170
Conclusion for Chapter 4 — 180

Conclusion — 182

Index — 184

Acknowledgements

I am thankful to a great many people for their help and support in writing this book, beyond those whom I can list here. However, certain people merit particular mention. I am grateful for the encouragement of a plethora of colleagues throughout this process, but particularly Geoff Pearson, Luke Graham, Margaret Cunningham, Ashley Hannay, Javier García Oliva and Jean d'Aspremont. I am also indebted to Yenkong Hodu who appointed me at the University of Manchester before this book was even conceived. Thanks must also go to my good friends and former colleagues Nic Ryder and James Kolaczkowski.

It is also important to acknowledge colleagues in the field of media law academia who offered advice and encouragement throughout the years. In particular, Pete Coe, Jacob Rowbottom, David Erdos, Rebecca Moosavian, Patrick O'Callaghan, Paul Wragg and David Rolph – thank you for welcoming me into the media law community with such kindness and grace. It is a pleasure to work alongside you in the broader media law community. The two people, though, to whom I am most grateful are Gavin Phillipson and Helen Fenwick. While they were originally my PhD supervisors, I am now privileged to call them friends. Without your training, knowledge, continued advice, unwavering advocacy and friendship this book would not have happened. It is hard to communicate the true depth of my gratitude. Thank you for the continued inspiration and counsel.

I also must extend a heartfelt thank you to Bristol University Press for their professionalism in publishing this book. Bristol University Press have made writing my first monograph a truly enjoyable and seamless experience. In particular, I would like to thank Helen Davis (who believed in this book before anyone), Grace Carroll and Zoe Forbes. Thank you for making this whole process a pleasure. I am also incredibly grateful to the 'OpenUp ECR Monograph' initiative, which has funded this book becoming open access. I am incredibly grateful.

Acknowledgement must also go to my closest friends, and in particular Siu-Yin Ho, Ian Hargreaves, Josh Sharp, Charlotte Barker, Megan Tang, Kat Lewis, Siobhan Smith, Anna Jobe and Michael Hutchinson. I would also like to thank my fellow 'band' of bellringers at St Mary the Virgin, Halkyn, and St Michael's, Shotwick: you provided a much needed outlet on difficult days.

Finally, though, my greatest and deepest vote of thanks must go to my family, who have always been (and continue to be) my biggest supporters. Thank you, Gill, Margaret and Timmy. I could not have done this without you.

Introduction

The world is currently in the grip of a technological revolution. This revolution began many years ago with the invention of the computer and worldwide web,[1] and progress towards a digital society shows no signs of stopping. In January 2025, UK Prime Minister Keir Starmer announced plans to integrate artificial intelligence (AI) into daily lives with a widespread program that will likely take many years, much new technology and a significant amount of personal data to achieve.[2] In the same month, the owners of social media giants Meta and X could be seen firmly seated at the front of Donald Trump's inauguration as the 47th President of the United States,[3] the US being UK's strongest international ally. Using the web to upload personal information about oneself or another is now commonplace. Facebook has 3,049 billion active users worldwide,[4] and

---

[1] The creation of the internet is widely considered to be 1 January 1983. For more information, see Jonathan Hogenback, 'Who invented the internet?', *Encyclopaedia Britannica* (13 June 2025) www.britannica.com/story/who-invented-the-internet and Ben Tarnoff, 'How the internet was invented' *The Guardian* (15 July 2016) www.theguardian.com/technology/2016/jul/15/how-the-internet-was-invented-1976-arpa-kahn-cerf accessed 29 January 2025.

[2] See 'PM speech on AI Opportunities Action Plan: 13 January 2025' (*GOV.UK*, 13 January 2025) www.gov.uk/government/speeches/pm-speech-on-ai-opportunities-action-plan-13-january-2025 accessed 29 January 2025.

[3] See 'Trump's inauguration: In pictures' (*BBC*, 21 January 2025) www.bbc.co.uk/news/resources/idt-e9bb4f21-518d-4242-a1b1-71250990e639 accessed 29 January 2025.

[4] Adam Connell, '22 leading social media platforms for 2025 (ranked by monthly active users)' (1 January 2025) https://adamconnell.me/social-media-platforms/ accessed 29 January 2025.

statisticians have estimated that 500 million posts per day are added to X (formerly Twitter).[5] The currency of social media – what makes it desirable, interesting and useable – is personal information. Particularly personal information that is in some way noteworthy, perhaps surprising or even salacious. Information can be easily repeated at the click of a button, being disseminated more widely and to new audiences, gathering yet more attention, engagement and clicks. Circa 2025, the technological horizon is rapidly changing – and has changed even in the last three years. Recent advancements in AI and machine learning have resulted in a plethora of AI- powered programs coming to the open market, many of which are free to use and even build.[6] Tools such as ChatGPT 4 – 'OpenAI's most advanced system' yet[7] – allowing a user to post question prompts to which they will receive answers.

Set against this backdrop, and perhaps because of it, more defamatory statements are now posted online than ever before. It is easy, free and instantaneous to upload a potentially defamatory post about another person online, reaching unfathomably large audiences such as X's 650 million users.[8] The potential such a post has to injure the reputation of those concerned is significant: the internet is the new medium of communication, with people now regularly consuming their

---

[5] Sarah Perez, 'Actually, "X sees 500M posts per day – not 100M–200M as Musk recently said"' (*TechCrunch*, 4 October 2024) https://techcrunch.com/2023/10/04/actually-x-sees-500m-posts-per-day-not-100m-200m-as-musk-recently-said/ accessed 29 January 2025.

[6] See, for example, Open AI: https://openai.com/ accessed 29 January 2025.

[7] Open AI, 'GPT-4 is OpenAI's most advanced system, producing safer and more useful responses' https://openai.com/index/gpt-4/ accessed 29 January 2025.

[8] See 'How many users on X? Statistics and facts (2025)' (*SEO.AI*, 21 January 2025) https://seo.ai/blog/how-many-users-on-x#:~:text=As%20of%20early%202025%2C%20X,reach%20up%20to%20300%20million accessed 29 January 2025.

news media using the web over more traditional sources such as televisions, books or papers.[9] If someone has been defamed on the web, word travels fast. Such a post could even 'go viral', when a seemingly innocuous post is distributed widely online in a short amount of time, attracting millions of viewers and wide engagement. Increasingly, politicians, public figures and world leaders are using the internet as a means of disseminating important information[10] – as such, defamatory posts online are no longer greeted with the scepticism they perhaps once were. The web is now seen as a place of perennial relevance and public debate. Consequently, many high-profile cases in English defamation law have been actioned pertaining to defamatory statements distributed on social media, such as *Vardy v Rooney*, *Blake v Fox* and *Riley v Murray*.[11]

Given the rise and seemingly unlimited potential for reputational devastation by defamation online, one would be forgiven for thinking that English law has taken robust steps to tackle this problem. Unfortunately for potential claimants, this is not the case. Quite the contrary, just over a decade ago the Defamation Act 2013 was passed, which has made bringing actions in defamation law more challenging in a number of ways. This reform was a result of pressure groups arguing that libel law had a 'chilling effect' on freedom of expression, resulting in a swing towards Article 10 European Convention

---

[9] Ishbel Macleod, 'Social media: The new era of news consumption' (*PA Media*, 16 October 2024) https://pa.media/blogs/editorial-data/social-media-the-new-era-of-news-consumption/#:~:text=More%20people%20use%20social%20media%20than%20BBC%20One%20to%20find%20news&text=The%20latest%20Ofcom%20news%20consumption,%25)%20noting%20declines%20from%202023 accessed 21 January 2025.

[10] See, for example, the UK Prime Minister's X account, 'UK Prime Minister @10downingstreet': https://x.com/10DowningStreet?ref_src=twsrc%5Egoogle%7Ctwcamp%5Eserp%7Ctwgr%5Eauthor accessed 29 January 2025.

[11] [2021] EWHC 1888; [2023] EWCA Civ 1000; [2022] EWCA Civ 1146.

on Human Rights (ECHR) interests as a result.[12] The central line of argument in this book is that more must be done in order to protect reputation, *ergo*, personal dignity, with respect to defamatory content posted to the web. This book will firstly consider the precise technological advancements which have prompted a crisis in online defamation. It will then move to evaluate what interest defamation law is actually protecting, using legal and philosophical theory in order to meaningfully articulate such an interest. Thirdly, it considers the status quo of English defamation law and notes barriers to redress for those defamed online, suggesting improvements to the law. In Chapter 4, this book argues that a remedy available under the UK (and EU) General Data Protection Regulation (GDPR) provides a better route to redress for those defamed online – the *'right to be forgotten'*.[13]

---

[12] Convention for the Protection of Human Rights and Fundamental Freedoms (4 November 1950, 3 September 1953) 005 CETS (ECHR). Alastair Mullis and Andrew Scott, 'The swing of the pendulum: Reputation, expression and the recentering of English libel law' (2012) 61(3) *Northern Ireland Legal Quarterly* 27.

[13] (UK) GDPR, Article 17.

ONE

Digital Advancements and Threats to Reputation

Introduction

Today it is truly a digital world. Technology both dominates and shapes society and, through its permeation in everyday lives, societal norms and patterns of behaviours are changing in ways which are measurable and susceptible to academic study.[1] It is now commonplace for an individual to use the internet from the moment they wake up until they go to sleep.[2] This chapter argues that the integration of sophisticated technology in daily lives has caused a fundamental societal shift to take place. This shift presents a greater threat to reputation rights than has been seen since the introduction of the printing press in the 15th century.

Rapid technological advancements have changed the global digital landscape. Advancements have come in the form of 'soft' mechanisms or applications, such as 'clouds', which can store vast amounts of information,[3] and 'hard' smart devices,

---

[1] Maryanne Wolf, 'Skim reading is the new normal: The effect on society is profound' *The Guardian* (25 August 2018) www.theguardian.com/commentisfree/2018/aug/25/skim-reading-new-normal-maryanne-wolf?utm_source=esp&utm_medium=Email&utm_cam%E2%80%A6 accessed 28 November 2022.

[2] One can use an app to 'find my phone' when it is lost, Google Maps to reach a meeting point with a friend and tell Alexa to switch off the lights.

[3] Using its subscription service, Apple offers up to 12 terabytes of storage on the iCloud, which is a vast amount of information, equivalent to up to

which are connected to wireless internet. Socio-economic changes have also had significant impact, in the form of readily affordable internet-enabled devices. It is now possible for many people to own a smartphone, tablet or laptop, easily depositing personal and damaging information about another online and viewing information posted by others. Social media is now intrinsically embodied in daily life. It is the new normal to post commentary about an event on X, to discuss oneself – or others – on LinkedIn and to post all manner of personal information about people we know on Facebook or Instagram. All of these websites are free to use at the most basic level. This personal information is then often backed up online, through the cloud.[4] There have been recent and rapid advancements in artificial intelligence (AI), such that it now seems poised to integrate within multiple aspects of private and public lives: chatbots are now able to have convincing conversations with the living, impersonating those in the 'real world' who are dead or alive.[5] Despite lukewarm early reviews of the 'Metaverse'[6] (financially backed by Facebook co-founder Mark Zuckerberg), parent company Meta appear determined to invest further in the online world and move society to a virtual platform. This online world allows individuals to socialize with one another through digital likenesses and even make speeches

---

a year of stored TikTok short videos: https://support.apple.com/en-gb/guide/icloud/mm3d17a80e23/icloud#:~:text=When%20you%20set%20up%20iCloud,or%2012%20TB%20of%20storage accessed 2 July 2025.

[4] For example the iCloud. See: www.icloud.com/ accessed 2 July 2025.

[5] See: 'Google fires software engineer who claims AI chatbot is sentient' *The Guardian* (23 July 2022) www.theguardian.com/technology/2022/jul/23/google-fires-software-engineer-who-claims-ai-chatbot-is-sentient accessed 1 July 2025.

[6] Tanya Basu, 'Meta is desperately trying to make the metaverse happen' *MIT Technology Review* (11 October 2022) www.technologyreview.com/2022/10/11/1061144/metaverse-announcements-meta-connect-legs/ accessed 1 July 2025.

and interact with virtual audiences – who represent real people operating through an online avatar.

Such advancements have led to a change in the way individuals view reputational interests and interact with the web, with many now regularly posting information about third parties. This shift to normalizing online disclosures has been compounded by the fact that the 'internet never forgets', as argued by Mayer-Schönberger.[7] This chapter will explain various technological advancements that have galvanized technology usage and led to a plethora of personal and potentially defamatory information deposited online. The chapter then considers specific threats to reputational interests as a result of these.

I. Technological advancements and threats to reputation

a. A beginning: the rise of cloud computing

Cloud computing is the single technological evolution that has shaped most of the digital world as it is now known. The innovation allowed modern advancements in IT,[8] yet experts claim it is still in its 'infancy',[9] with much more capability yet to be seen. Cloud computing is the backbone that supports many digital capabilities, such as the aggregation of personal data, the Internet of Things, AI and social media websites.[10] A working definition of cloud computing is 'on-demand network access to a shared pool of configurable computing resources'.[11] Cloud computing means that 'simple portals'

---

[7] Viktor Mayer-Schönberger, *Delete: The Virtue of Forgetting in the Digital Age* (Princeton University Press 2009).
[8] Nayan B. Ruparelia, *Cloud Computing* (MIT Press 2016) 3.
[9] Ibid.
[10] Ali Sunyaev, *Internet Computing: Principles of Distributed Systems and Emerging Internet-Based Technologies* (Springer 2020).
[11] Ibid 4. This is a shortened version of the National Institute of Standards and Technology's definition in the US.

can be used to log in to the cloud, a virtual space where data can be stored and shared. This virtual space can be accessed from any number of devices, anywhere.[12] Ruparelia calls this 'ubiquitous computing' and notes that this concept was initially promulgated by universities.[13] Indeed, Facebook initially began as a website called 'Facemash' where a cycle of photographs of two different Harvard attendees were pitted against each other, with a user deciding which of the individuals were more attractive.[14]

The cloud is readily available as it exists in the online space whether users are engaging or not.[15] As such, time and location have lost their previous importance as information can be accessed from any web-enabled place, at any time.[16] Cloud service models are also varied and diverse.[17] Clouds can be personal, social, financial or can be a cloud of 'things'.[18] Oppitz and Tomsu have argued that cloud computing is a 'global service ecosystem' and cannot be explained with reference to the binary understanding of private or public spaces; rather, it is 'a hybrid area where new rules are developed and changed quickly'.[19] The capacity of the cloud to store ever-increasing amounts of information continues to grow,[20]

---

[12] Ibid 5–17.

[13] Ruparelia (n 8) 63.

[14] Katharine Kaplan, 'Facemash creator survives ad board' *The Crimson. com* (19 November 2003) https://web.archive.org/web/20190504172812/www.thecrimson.com/article/2003/11/19/facemash-creator-survives-ad-board-the/ accessed 28 November 2023.

[15] Sunyaev (n 10) 17.

[16] Marcus Oppitz and Peter Tomsu, *Inventing the Cloud Century: How Cloudiness Keeps Changing Our Life, Economy and Technology* (Springer 2018) 412.

[17] Sunyaev (n 10) 207.

[18] Ibid 56 and see Federica Cappelletti, Alessandra Papetti, Marta Rossi and Michele Germani 'Smart strategies for household food waste management' (2022) 200 *Procedia Computer Science* 887.

[19] Oppitz and Tomsu (n 16) 411.

[20] Ibid 414.

giving users the seemingly endless ability to promulgate true (or false) personal information about others. To add further complexity, the cloud is virtual and therefore 'borderless', going beyond the boundaries of countries or, arguably, social class.[21] It is also possible to create a 'societal cloud' – a service provided to a group that has common purposes or goals. Ruparelia gives the example of a cloud for NATO, as clouds can easily service big data sets due to their ephemeral nature.[22] Posting information or media utilizing such a cloud could reach an unimaginable amount of people. As such, cloud uses can range from mass scale to small scale, with the cloud harbouring material that could reach large or more modest audiences.

i. Cloud computing and threats to reputation

In summary, the cloud makes information sharing on a grand scale possible. Indeed, it makes it easy, fast and convenient to spread misinformation or false and defamatory information.[23] For this key reason, cloud computing has enabled defamation of individuals on a previously unheard-of scale. Defamatory content can be remotely uploaded to the cloud by any user who has login credentials; all one would need is a relatively basic device connected to the internet, such as a smartphone. The cloud could then be used to further share this information to a myriad of other users through its wireless connectivity capability. The cloud's ability to store large amounts of information – be it true or false, accurate or inaccurate – is the reason that social media websites and other such sites (discussed later in this chapter) can function in the way that they do. Cloud computing as a system therefore *enables and allows for*

---

[21] Ibid 411.
[22] Ruparelia (n 8) 54–5.
[23] Oppitz and Tomsu (n 16) 413.

large-scale defamation of an individual to take place online. This can be seen as the single salient development, much like the printing press, that has changed the global reputational landscape. Before the digital revolution which is currently gripping the world, it would be hard to imagine reputational damage of this scale or magnitude. In the 1980s, when the ruthless UK tabloid press was in its heyday (leading to a new interest in the details of private lives)[24] legal professionals and those wishing to safeguard information rights raised concerns. Despite these issues, impacts on reputations were necessarily limited by the scale of the physical publication of paper copies of newspapers in the 1980s and 1990s. Due to the sheer ease in storing and disseminating false personal information made possible by clouds, the potential for mass libel on a previously unseen scale is now here, dwarfing concerns over the printing press of years past.

A further concern is the power that lies behind cloud computing. As clouds continue to grow and develop, it is likely that the control behind key enterprises will be consolidated into the hands of one or two parent companies.[25] This in turn makes it increasingly easy for such a conglomerate, if they wished, to influence public opinion for a range of nefarious purposes,[26] for example by supplying potentially incorrect information about an individual to a third-party source, such as a government.[27] Extremist groups can also take advantage of the cloud to spread propaganda or hate about an individual, based on false and defamatory information.[28]

---

[24] See Jacob Rowbottom, 'Kaye v Robertson [1991] FSR 62' in Paul Wragg and Peter Coe (eds), *Landmark Cases in Privacy Law* (Hart 2023) 90ff.
[25] Ruparelia (n 8) 229–30.
[26] Ibid 229–33.
[27] Ibid.
[28] Oppitz and Tomsu (n 16) 418–19.

b. The birth of social media

For the purposes of this book, one of the most significant developments since the early 2000s is the rise of social media. The first widely adopted social media website reaching a world audience was Myspace, which launched in 2003. By 2005, Myspace had 16 million regular users and it was the most successful social media site between 2005 and 2008.[29] It blended social networking with music and hosted personalized landing pages containing a plethora of personal information that was easy to update, such as photo caches, preferred choices of music and a list of 'top friends' who corresponded to real-world individuals who also had accounts on the site. Media such as photographs could be engaged with using comments appearing below an image. In an example of how the digital can impact real-world relationships offline, people were encouraged to rank their on-site 'friends' in what one can only assume was an order of preference for all to see. Myspace could be used to send or post messages containing information about oneself or others. Landing pages were also very customizable, with various themes and wallpapers downloadable from other free sites, while 'arrival music' played when one clicked on a user's profile.

Myspace can be seen as a primary influence or trailblazer for all subsequent developments in social media. Facebook also contained a similar personalized landing page, although with less emphasis on music and more emphasis on posting information about oneself or others through 'wall posts'. Myspace is still credited with beginning the burgeoning rise of social media among young people, by branding itself as an 'edgy' destination people could connect with music artists and friends.[30] After the early success of Myspace,

---

[29] *Encyclopaedia Britannica*, 'Myspace: Web site' (10 November 2023) www.britannica.com/topic/Myspace accessed 1 July 2025.
[30] Ibid.

social networking sites online have thrived, continuing to grow and expand in popularity. Myspace was eventually deposed by Facebook as the world's most popular social networking site in 2009. Facebook branded itself as a site that predominantly connected friends and family members, with a less fashionable USP than Myspace, which was seen by some as having an element of counterculture. As such, Facebook has been more successful in capturing a broader age range of users. As of 2023, approximately 10 per cent of Facebook users were 65 years old or over. Circa 2025 a further shift occurred and young people (who perhaps would previously have been caught in Myspace's orbit) now predominantly engage with image- or video-based social media websites. This includes YouTube, TikTok, Instagram and Snapchat.[31] All of these sites use short- or long-form video content and images to communicate information to large or small audiences. TikTok, Instagram and Snapchat in particular prioritize short clip sharing as the primary method that information is disseminated on the sites, such as 'stories' on Snapchat.[32] Direct engagement between users happens in public comment sections or private messages, which are available on each of the sites, all of which have 'apps' for ease

---

[31] See Emily A. Vogels, Risa Gelles-Watnick and Navid Massarat, 'Teens, social media and technology 2022' (*Pew Research Centre*, 10 August 2022) www.pewresearch.org/internet/2022/08/10/teens-social-media-and-technology-2022/#:~:text=YouTube%20stands%20out%20as%20the,%25)%20and%20Snapchat%20(59%25 accessed 8 April 2024. Also see: www.youtube.com/; www.tiktok.com/en/; www.instagram.com/; www.snapchat.com/ accessed 2 July 2025.

[32] See, for example, Aliaksandra Shutsko, 'User-generated short video content in social media: A case study of TikTok' in *Social Computing and Social Media. Participation, User Experience, Consumer Experience, and Applications of Social Computing*, Proceedings of the 12th International Conference (Springer 2020), SCSM 2020, Held as Part of the 22nd HCI International Conference, HCII 2020, Copenhagen, July 2020), Proceedings, Part II, 108.

of use on smartphones. However, purely text-based social media posts are still utilized – for example, YouTube has a 'community' section that acts like a noticeboard where users, using 'channels', can write text comments if they wish. Due to this shift in *type* of social media that is now being widely consumed, claimants may see a rise in potentially defamatory information shared by short video.

ii. Social media and threats to reputation

In the internet age, defamation through social media websites is now not only commonplace but is quickly becoming one of the most prevalent methods by which individuals are defamed in England and Wales. The case of *Stocker v Stocker* reached the Supreme Court in 2019 and argued that the respondent had been defamed through a Facebook exchange stating 'he tried to strangle me'.[33] Three of the most high-profile defamation cases of 2023 and 2024, *Hay v Cresswell*, *Aaronson v Stones* and *Blake v Fox*, concerned defamation through social media.[34] It seems that the transition to the digital era has now been completed and that if one is to be defamed, social media is now a likely form by which this will happen. As will be discussed at length later in this book, this change in medium is causing problems for judges in navigating the complexities of such sites, the extent of audience engagement with the source and whether to take such posts as seriously as those in the traditional print media.[35] English defamation law, with a vast case-law history and roots in the Roman law of *injuria*, is now expected to adapt.

---

[33] [2019] UKSC 17 [1]–[4].
[34] [2023] EWHC 882 (KB); [2023] EWHC 2399 (KB); [2024] EWHC 956 (KB).
[35] For example, which may be considered when evaluating the satisfaction of s 1 Defamation Act 2013.

Long before *Stocker* was decided in 2019, those keenly observing legal developments could see a gradual trend towards defamatory content appearing not only in print, but online – the famous line of decisions in *Flood v Times Newspapers* between 2009 and 2012 drew discussion from the judiciary in the High Court regarding the status of *The Times* website publication,[36] which remained accessible after the print version of the article had gone out of circulation and factual circumstances had changed.[37] Although *Flood* did not specifically concern a *social media* website, herein lies a profound concern for those defamed via social media: the longevity of the post itself. Unless the person who has made the post on social media manually removes it, or the host of the website seeks the post out and deletes it, the defamatory information has the potential to remain on that site forever, cemented into the annals of internet history. This concern has become so widespread that s 5 of the Defamation Act 2013 was enacted to protect operators of websites against a slew of claims that could be potentially actioned against them for defamatory content on their websites, posted by third-party individuals.[38] Aside from the indefinite timeframe that a defamatory post on a social media can be potentially visible, another central factor in the damaging nature of defamation by social media is the global reach of such websites. Facebook has a worldwide audience – statisticians estimate 2.9 billion active users – and if posts are public, there is the potential they can be seen by those who do not even subscribe to the website.[39] This was

---

[36] *Flood v Times Newspapers* [2009] EWHC 2375 (QB), [2010] EWCA Civ 804, [2012] UKSC 11.

[37] [2009] EWHC 2375 (QB) [H11.6].

[38] This will be discussed in Chapter 3, Part II.

[39] 'Leading countries based on Facebook audience size as of January 2024' *Statista* (2024) www.statista.com/statistics/268136/top-15-countries-based-on-number-of-facebook-users/#:~:text=With%20around%20 2.9%20billion%20monthly,most%20popular%20social%20media%20wo rldwide accessed 10 April 2024.

also the case until 2023 for Twitter/X, while YouTube is predominantly public. If one is defamed via a social media website, there is a real potential the statement can go national or 'viral'. A further harming facet of defamation through social media is that engagement with the defamatory post is encouraged. People leave comments and discuss issues on YouTube videos, some videos amassing hundreds of thousands of comments on a single post, with thousands of 'upvotes' and replies. TikTok operates a system where a user can link to a previous video post and respond directly with a video of their own, or respond to a comment using a video.[40] This can lead to further promulgation of the defamatory content and even the generation of new reputationally harmful material.

c. Wide availability of technology

In addition to digital innovations, socio-economic changes have also shaped the modern technological landscape. As such, the ease of access to technology is a significant contributing factor towards increased threats to reputation. In 2025, 95 per cent of the population have a smartphone, a product characterized by internet access.[41] This rapid increase in ownership of internet-enabled devices means that it is quick and convenient to deposit personal information about others on the internet, be it on social media or another type

---

[40] 'Product tutorial: Reply to comments with video' (*TikTok.com*, 18 June 2020) https://newsroom.tiktok.com/en-us/product-tutorial-reply-to-comments-with-video accessed 10 April 2024.

[41] Catherine Hiley, 'UK mobile phone statistics, 2022' (*Uswitch*, 30 September 2022) www.uswitch.com/mobiles/studies/mobile-statistics/#:~:text=A%20breakdown%20of%20UK%20age,78%25%20aged%2055%20and%20above accessed 28 November 2022. Also see Matthew Boyle and Sophie Barber, 'Mobile phone and internet usage statistics in the UK' (*Finder.com*, 4 July 2025) https://www.finder.com/uk/banking/mobile-internet-statistics accessed 24 July 2025.

of website. Sophisticated technology is also increasingly portable: a smartphone can comfortably sit in a pocket and a laptop or tablet can be easily transported around the country or globe. In the aftermath of the COVID-19 pandemic, many employers have now embraced a 'hybrid' working policy,[42] leading to the workforce having increasing amounts of technological hardware at home and engaging with a wider degree of software which often requires the input of personal information about oneself or others.[43] This normality of access to technology engenders prevalence – technology is now everywhere and seemingly used by everyone, and it is increasingly societally acceptable to discuss others in public settings online.

As alluded to, the affordable price of web-enabled technology has contributed to its wide uptake. As of 2025, certain smartphones in the UK are available to purchase at under £100.[44] A broader social demographic is therefore able to purchase and use such products, while a highly competitive market with a large range of computers, tablets and smartphones acts to drive prices down.[45] This generally accepted – and expected – usage of technology circa 2025 is

---

[42] The Office for National Statistics (ONS) has reported that even after COVID restrictions were lifted, as of February 2022, eight out of ten workers still planned to work partly from home. See 'Is hybrid working here to stay?' (*ONS*, 23 May 2022) www.ons.gov.uk/employmentandlabourmarket/peopleinwork/employmentandemployeetypes/articles/ishybridworkingheretostay/2022-05-23 accessed 28 November 2022.

[43] For example, Microsoft Teams, providing an online workspace and meeting place. See www.microsoft.com/en-ww/microsoft-teams/teams-for-work accessed 28 November 2022.

[44] See for example Tesco selling the 'moto e14' at under £100: https://www.tesco.com/phones/products/00840023268229 accessed 14 August 2025.

[45] On cursory examination, British electrical retailer Currys has an online offering of nearly 500 laptops and nearly 260 tablets. See

due to changing societal norms in the digital era. The general social response to rapid technological advancements has been to embrace them,[46] as evidenced by the rise in technology usage. It is increasingly common to document life events online to a potentially global audience;[47] uploading a photo or a text-based post to Instagram is a new form of social interaction.[48] Early studies have shown that individuals in Generation Z do not read information in the same way as previous generations: 'skim reading' has become default as information is now primarily consumed online, where data is widely shared through image-based content.[49] As such, the shift looks set to become yet more significant as Gen Z, born into such technology, grow into adulthood.

The role of internet-based technology is now so significant it dominates world affairs of the most crucial kind. A pertinent example is Starlink, a 'satellite Internet constellation' from company Space X.[50] The idea behind Starlink is to provide internet access more readily and efficiently to both areas that do not have coverage and to ones that do; the aim of the scheme is 'providing global Internet access'.[51] It is arguably the most widescale current development in communications

---

www.currys.co.uk/computing/ipad-tablets-and-ereaders/tablets accessed 28 November 2022.

[46] Although this embrace may not always yield positive outcomes. See Shaohai Jiang and Annabel Ngien, 'The effects of Instagram use, social comparison, and self-esteem on social anxiety: A survey study in Singapore' (2020) *Social Media + Society* 1.

[47] See picture- (and video)-sharing social media site, Instagram: www.instagram.com/ accessed 2 July 2025.

[48] Soo-Hyun Jun, 'Why do people post photos on Instagram?' (2022) 14(12648) *Sustainability* 1.

[49] Ibid 2 and Wolf (n 1).

[50] Tong Duan and Venkata Dinavahi, 'Starlink space network-enhanced cyber-physical power system' (2021) 12(4) *EEE Transactions on Smart Grid* 3673.

[51] Ibid 3673.

technology, and began around 2015.[52] The role of Starlink has already proved impactful on the world stage in the context of the Russian invasion of Ukraine in February 2022. On request from a Ukrainian political official (via Twitter, as it then was), Elon Musk responded that Starlink had unofficially launched over Ukraine, providing the country with satellite internet connection.[53] As of April 2022, Starlink had 10,000 dishes in service, with more expected, and the ability to provide internet access to the most rural of areas.[54] Experts have commented that this has been a 'salvation' – the launch of the project was doubtlessly impressive, despite being a 'mad dash'.[55] This is a further example of how society now ceases to function without internet access, even in wartime. In our homes, it is now a mains service, similar to electricity, gas and water.

iii. Affordable technology and threats to reputation

As explained, the prevalence of technological hardware due to wide affordability means that now most people in the UK have access to an internet-enabled device. The impact of this is that wide-scale communication of defamatory information about another can originate from anyone, at any time, through the medium of the internet. It is now within most people's capabilities to utilize a smartphone to log into a social media website – to which it is free to sign up – and post false and potentially defamatory information about another.

---

[52] Ibid.
[53] Kevin Collier, 'Starlink internet becomes a lifeline for Ukrainians' (*NBC News*, 29 April 2022) www.nbcnews.com/tech/security/elon-musks-starlink-internet-becomes-lifeline-ukrainians-rcna25360 accessed 2 July 2025.
[54] Ibid and Duan and Dinavahi (n 50).
[55] Collier (n 53).

This is not the case in the mainstream printed press, such as newspapers: in order that a potentially defamatory story can be run about an individual, the story would have to pass a wide variety of checking points or hurdles, from the person who wrote the story to their line manager, to eventually the editor of the newspaper and the legal team – before the story reached print. This is in contrast to modern technology, which links anyone who can afford a web-enabled device directly to the internet. Everyone now has the ability to publish defamatory content to a potentially wide audience without any form of editorial oversight.[56] This also means that the likely subjects of defamation have changed; in the past, through tabloid press culture, well-known faces were much more likely to be the target subjects of potentially defamatory publications. In 2025 a much wider array of targets are likely, apart from the rich and famous – as people with a myriad of personal and private vendettas are capable of uploading defamatory statements. This links to the concept of posts going viral; noteworthy online posts may generate a wide range interest, far beyond the intended or even expected audience. These instances may well relate to private individuals, rather than celebrities. An example is a recording of a parish council meeting in Handforth, a small civil parish in Cheshire, UK, which went viral in 2021, with videos and clips from the meeting amassing millions of views on YouTube.[57]

---

[56] This is, of course, notwithstanding that many social media and other websites have a terms of service policy. See for example, Facebook's policy, https://en-gb.facebook.com/legal/terms accessed 15 April 2024. Posts can, of course, be taken down by site moderators due to improper usage.

[57] See, for example, this clip of the 'best parts' www.youtube.com/watch?v=zy3Kml-F7J0 and *The Guardian*'s post of the meeting: www.youtube.com/watch?v=l17UIwAFOyk accessed 15 April 2024.

With this increased access to sophisticated technology has come newfound normality in discussing what may have previously been private conversations in public settings on social media websites. It is now the norm to share personal feelings or information about another in a public setting on sites such as Facebook or Twitter/X and, indeed, many defamation cases have arisen pertaining to both sites to date.[58] This shift has led to a situation where posting about another on the internet is not viewed as an unusual thing to do, resulting in yet more potential for defamatory statements to flood the internet. Early studies have shown that a desire to 'belong' can even encourage certain patterns of behaviour on social media sites.[59] Due to the large amount of personal information shared on a daily basis online,[60] it is even possible to foresee unintentional but nevertheless defamatory statements issued on the internet through a post by an individual to their own page, predominantly about themselves – but also containing potentially defamatory content about others. The more one posts on social media, the more incentives there are to continue posting. On YouTube, when an account reaches 1,000 'subscribers' that channel becomes 'monetized' and suitable for companies to place advertisements on. The people behind the YouTube channels then receive monthly 'adsense' payments which correlate to how often the

---

[58] See Kirsty Horsey and Erika Rackley, *Tort Law* (OUP 2023) ch 17 – websites: (*Godfrey v Demon Internet* [2001] QB 201), tweets: (*McAlpine; Monroe v Hopkins* [2017] EWHC 433 (QB)), blogs: (*Cruddas v Adams* [2013] EWHC 145 (QB)), Facebook (*Stocker v Stocker* [2019] UKSC 17, *Hay v Cresswell* [2023] EWHC 882 (KB)).

[59] Christiane M. Büttner, Fanny Lalot and Selma C. Rudert, 'Showing with whom I belong: The desire to belong publicly on social media' (2023) 139 *Computers in Human Behaviour* 107535.

[60] It was estimated that, worldwide, people spent on average 143 minutes per day on social media in 2024. See 'Daily time spent on social networking by internet users worldwide from 2012 to 2025' (*Statista*, 19 June 2025) www.statista.com/statistics/433871/daily-social-media-usage-worldwide/ accessed 2 July 2025.

video (and therefore advertisements) are viewed. To grow a social media account, advisors argue that there should be an emphasis on creating posts that will be further shared.[61] With this increased traffic of content comes an increased likelihood of defamatory statements as transmitted online. Indeed, the more salacious or controversial the content of a website, the more traffic (and therefore more money) this can drive to a channel and its owners.

Finally, internet-enabled technology also allows an individual to post online *anonymously*. It is straightforward to sign up to a social media website with false details, using an email account that one can easily again obtain with any form of false information. Hiding behind an online pseudonym in order to defame someone is an attractive prospect to potential defamers – as particularly those with malicious intent may feel safe from persecution through an anonymous online persona. As will be discussed later in this book, this in turn makes bringing an action against such an individual difficult, although the annexed statutory instrument to the s 5 defence for operators of websites in the Defamation Act 2013 can be successful at finding a middle ground in such situations.[62]

d. The 'Metaverse' and online worlds

Beyond advancements in hardware and internet access, companies are now striving to take technology one step further

---

[61] Brendan Kane, 'How I gained one million followers' in *One Million Followers* (BenBella Books 2018).

[62] In such a case, if personal details of the poster are not forthcoming, the website will remove the content within five days to avoid themselves being actioned against in defamation. See The Defamation (Operators of Websites) Regulations 2013, UK Statutory Instruments, 2013 No 3028 www.legislation.gov.uk/uksi/2013/3028/contents/made accessed 26 August 2024.

and develop virtual *worlds*. Facebook parent company Meta has invested a significant amount of money building such a world – the 'Metaverse'.[63] The Metaverse has the aim of creating a fully functioning in-world ecosystem. It hosts digital marketplaces using cryptocurrency and supplemented by the trading of NFTs (non-fungible tokens),[64] but more crucially – as far as this monograph is concerned – builds social spaces for users to interact with one another and allows individuals to embody avatars in an entirely online augmented reality.[65] When users log on, they choose their avatar and then are greeted with a landing page, or a 'safe zone', where people cannot interact with them – however, after a user navigates away from this, they then enter various virtual community spaces where they will interact with others, also embodying avatars. Information can be communicated between avatars in various ways; people can use microphones or text-based comments in order to speak to one another, or make speeches to potentially large audiences of other avatars, all of whom have real people behind them.[66]

---

[63] Reportedly $36 billion dollars. See Jyoti Mann, 'Meta has spent $36 billion building the metaverse but still has little to show for it, while tech sensations such as the iPhone, Xbox, and Amazon Echo cost way less' (*Insider*, 29 October 2022) www.businessinsider.com/meta-lost-30-bill ion-on-metaverse-rivals-spent-far-less-2022-10?r=US&IR=T#:~:text= Meta%20has%20spent%20%2436%20billion,Amazon%20Echo%20c ost%20way%20less accessed 2 July 2025.

[64] Academics have argued that conceptions of property are changing due to the move to 'Web3' and online worlds. See Russell Belk, Mariam Humayun and Myriam Brouard, 'Money, possessions, and ownership in the Metaverse: NFTs, cryptocurrencies, Web3 and wild markets' (2022) 153 *Journal of Business Research* 198.

[65] Peter Weber, 'How Facebook's metaverse could change your life' (*The Week*, 28 November 2021) https://theweek.com/facebook/1007 409/how-facebooks-metaverse-could-change-your-life accessed 2 July 2025.

[66] See the video made by RT Game, 'I played Facebook's VR Metaverse so you don't have to' (*YouTube*, 30 October 2022) www.youtube.com/ watch?v=UdqrFa6pWLA accessed 16 April 2024.

Access using a virtual reality headset gives users an even more immersive, whole-body experience,[67] where they see the Metaverse as if it appeared directly in front of them and can hold controllers in each hand to give the sensation of physically interacting with both people and things in the virtual world. One can move towards and 'touch' other avatars, while objects in the virtual world can be picked up or otherwise interacted with. While some initial responses to early versions of the Metaverse have been lukewarm,[68] Meta continues to develop the project, particularly as potential for growth has been seen for the product in the gaming industry market.[69] Forbes continues to consider the Metaverse a worthwhile financial investment, partly because it allows advertisers to reach target audiences in new and increasingly diverse ways.[70] Aside from the Metaverse, other virtual worlds have long existed online where individuals can interact and communicate with each other using virtual shared spaces, such as VRChat,[71] which has over 25,000 virtual worlds.[72] Furthermore, virtual reality hardware is not required to engage (opening to the experience to a larger demographic). As such, advancements in digital world building show no signs of stopping.

---

[67] See the playthrough in the video (n 66). An example of such a headset is the Oculus Rift: www.oculus.com/rift-s/?locale=en_GB accessed 27 August 2024.

[68] Ibid.

[69] 'Metaverse development complete guide: What you need to know about the Metaverse in 2024' (*TokenMinds*, 21 December 2023) https://tokenminds.co/blog/metaverse-development/metaverse-development accessed 16 April 2024.

[70] Andrew Michael and Kevin Pratt, 'How to invest in the Metaverse' *Forbes* (29 November 2022) www.forbes.com/uk/advisor/investing/how-to-invest-in-the-metaverse/ accessed 2 July 2025.

[71] See the VRChat website: https://hello.vrchat.com/. The game is accessible through the 'Steam' shop for computer gamers.

[72] Ibid.

iv. Online worlds and threats to reputation

Much as in the real world, a virtual world can be used to disseminate defamatory content about another individual, to large or small audiences – as of 2024, it was estimated that there are 400 million active users of the Metaverse.[73] One can foresee the usage of avatars leading to an increase in individuals revealing compromising – and potentially defamatory – information about another in a range of different ways. It is clear that revealing reputationally damaging personal information to a group of other avatars (or people) in a virtual world clearly satisfies the publication requirement for one to be defamed in the eyes of others in English law, although if this would satisfy the serious harm threshold necessary to bring a claim in s 1(1) of the Defamation Act 2013 remains to be seen and would depend, for example, on the potential reach of the information.[74] Information could be delivered in a slanderous capacity through speaking words through a microphone to real-world listeners behind other avatars, or libel could be committed by writing something that would be included in an online world – such as a virtual community noticeboard – in a more permanent form.[75] As one is shielded by an anonymous avatar, this may increase willingness to disseminate spurious, damaging and false information about another, as a user may feel that they would be less likely to experience repercussions.

---

[73] Josh Howarth, '75+ Metaverse statistics (new 2024 data)' (*Exploding Topics*, 22 November 2023) https://explodingtopics.com/blog/metaverse-stats accessed 16 April 2024.

[74] *Lachaux v Independent Print* [2019] UKSC 27 [21], where Lord Sumption noted, much like Mr Justice Warby before him, that the 'scale of publications' was relevant to whether the s 1 threshold was met.

[75] The importance between the traditional distinction between libel and slander has been eroded due to the introduction of the serious harm threshold in s 1 Defamation Act 2013. Traditionally, libel takes a more

As can be expected, there are a multitude of legal issues with the potential to culminate in the Metaverse (or any other virtual world). Cheong has considered whether a 'veil' should be lifted in certain circumstances to reveal who is behind an avatar,[76] although it is as yet unclear what type of law would apply in an instance whereby one avatar infringed the reputational rights of another, or whether an avatar could have legal responsibility.[77] A veil of an avatar could perhaps be lifted in order that the user be held accountable for civil offences such as defamation – much like legal systems pierce the corporate veil to hold those behind companies responsible, despite companies having separate legal personalities.[78] If an avatar is incorporated, this could lead to an action being brought against the avatar itself,[79] although it is unclear how this would work in practice or if this is desirable from the perspective of legal experts. Short of removing defamatory information from the 'virtual world' (which presumably would be a comparatively achievable fix), a claimant would be unlikely to receive damages – monetary compensation – from an avatar who has no independent financial wealth. The Metaverse will also generate new forms of 'personal' data, specific to an avatar, leading to further questions about the application of supranational data protection instruments such as the General Data Protection Regulation,[80] which could also potentially be used to remove defamatory personal information online, as will be discussed later in this book.

---

permanent form than slander and is therefore actionable per se. See, for example, *Monson v Tussauds Ltd* [1894] 1 QB 671.

[76] Ben Chester Cheong, 'Avatars in the metaverse: Potential legal issues and remedies' (2022) 3 *International Cybersecurity Law Review* 1.

[77] Ibid 4.

[78] Ibid 15.

[79] Ibid 21.

[80] Dependant, of course, on this information as classified as personal data. Ibid 25.

Cheong also argues that the potential to hide behind an avatar could lead to people committing acts online that they would not ordinarily commit.[81]

e. Augmented reality

Linked to the Metaverse, another technology trend that has gathered pace is the rise of augmented reality. This is where (for example) a phone application generates a display that represents – in part – the real world, with virtual elements overlaid in order that the display can largely appear real, and where one can interact with it. The reality is 'augmented' because the superimposed parts are 'generated by a computer' and are not real.[82] Despite being a concept first debuted in the 1960s,[83] the trend has only recently begun to dominate the mobile app market, such that Apple have dedicated webpages extoling the virtues of using virtual reality applications on their devices, iPads, iMacs and iPhones.[84] A few of the application examples given by Apple on these webpages include games, but also photography apps and – crucially – social media apps such as 'Snapchat', where the 'reality' of pictures can be superimposed upon. Pokémon GO is an example of an app that was a popular sensation that harnessed real-world locations and user whereabouts as crucial to the game. Pokémon GO uses augmented reality as it blends the real world and the

---

[81] Ibid 6.
[82] Raffaele Vertucci, Salvatore D'Onofrio, Stefano Ricciardi and Maurizio De Nino, 'History of augmented reality' in Andrew Yeh Ching Nee and Soh Khim Ong (eds), *Springer Handbook of Augmented Reality* (Springer 2023) 35.
[83] Ibid.
[84] 'Augmented reality' (*Apple.com*) www.apple.com/uk/augmented-reality/ accessed 29 November 2023.

digital world.[85] The technology that supports augmented reality programs is 'simple',[86] leading to such apps becoming increasingly commonplace. The technology that supports augmented reality is also relatively low cost, even if one wants a wearable piece of hardware which displays the altered reality, such as Google Glass.[87]

v. Augmented reality and threats to reputation

When one considers reputation rights, augmented reality is a particularly concerning technological advancement as it hinges on the ability to blur lines between what is true and what is false. If someone cannot be certain what they are seeing is real – and if it is in fact only partly real – it is easy to foresee eventualities where, for example, videos of individuals are taken out of context and clipped into other convincing 'realities', changing the nature of what is said or done, to the reputational detriment of those concerned. For example, a pre-existing picture of a person in a compromising position could be overlayed virtually to a real-world environment, implying, for example, moral disrepute. Even if a defamatory imputation was not explicit, defamation by innuendo could potentially mean there was liability for such an augmented picture if a defamatory meaning was implied, for example by 'reading between the lines' or relying on extraneous facts known to an audience.[88] Consider a

---

[85] Diana Martinez, 'Counteracting diminished privacy in an augmented reality: Protecting geolocation privacy' (2017) 50(4) *Loyola of Los Angeles Law Review* 713, 715.

[86] Ibid 715.

[87] Vertucci et al (n 82) 35.

[88] See, for example, *Lewis v Daily Telegraph* [1964] AC 234 (false innuendo, reading between the lines to infer the defamatory meaning); *The Lord McAlpine of West Green v Sally Bercow (No 2)* [2013] EWHC 1342 (true innuendo, deduced by knowledge of extraneous facts).

scenario where a computer-generated likeness of an individual could be superimposed virtually over a real-world environment, such as footage of a brothel. As technology progresses, it may become difficult to distinguish which aspects of an image or footage are real and which computer generated, particularly as augmented reality mixes medias (and people may assume that because some of what they are seeing is clearly real, all other aspects are also).

Partly because of its simplicity and the low economic cost of engagement, technology experts have warned that augmented reality is a 'disruptive technology' with the potential to transform the world in a significant way. Vertucci et al observe that 'AR [will] deeply transform the world of work, the way we interact with others, and the society in general.'[89] Laws internationally have been slow to keep up with technological developments in the field,[90] and there are also counter-arguments to strict legal regulation, such as that augmented reality can aid crime prevention.[91]

f. Artificial intelligence

The current technological climate is dominated by developments in AI. The field has been researched in academia and developed in industry since the 1970s and its prevalence has recently gathered pace and media attention.[92] Despite vast amounts of academic discourse on AI, an agreed-upon definition is

---

[89] Vertucci et al (n 82) 36.
[90] For a discussion of this as the technology became emergent in the US, see Kevin F. King, 'Personal jurisdiction, internet commerce, and privacy: The pervasive legal consequences of modern geolocation technologies' (2011) 21 *Albany Law Journal of Science & Technology* 61, 116.
[91] Elena Militello, 'Geolocation in crime detection and prevention' in Lorena Bachmaier Winter and Stefano Ruggeri (eds), *Investigating and Preventing Crime in the Digital Era* (Springer 2022).
[92] See, for example, Earl B. Hunt, *Artificial Intelligence* (Academic Press 1975).

elusive – Hunt has argued that the term relates to machine problem solving, learning and decision making, among other hallmarks.[93] There is a range of different types and levels of AI: 'strong AI' mimics human levels of intelligence.[94] In 2022, it was reported that Google had dismissed senior software engineer Blake Lemoine who was working on a project concerning AI chatbot LaMDA.[95] Lemoine had expressed to executives at Google (and later the media) that he believed LaMDA was in fact sentient and had the same capacity for interaction as an eight-year-old child due to the nature of the conversations he had conducted with the bot, including ones about personhood.[96] It is not a stretch to imagine individuals cultivating meaningful personal relationships with AI chatbots and revealing private information about themselves, be it true or false, which in turn could be used to publicly humiliate them. Websites which cultivate AI chatbots are thriving. The website 'character.ai' hosts an enormous number of character AI-powered chatbots with whom millions of real people are conversing on a daily basis.[97] The range of characters available to speak with is large; ranging from fictional character Sherlock Holmes, who has 6.7 million 'chats', to bots mimicking *real individuals*, such as a chatbot with a striking resemblance to tech entrepreneur Elon Musk, who has had over 35.1 million 'chats'.[98] These numbers demonstrate the wealth of engagement

---

[93] Ibid 3.
[94] Konrad Szocik and Agata Jurkowska-Gomułka, 'Ethical, legal and political challenges of artificial intelligence: Law as a response to AI-related threats and hopes' (2021) *World Futures* 1, 2.
[95] 'Google fires software engineer who claims AI chatbot is sentient' *The Guardian* (23 July 2022) www.theguardian.com/technology/2022/jul/23/google-fires-software-engineer-who-claims-ai-chatbot-is-sentient accessed 2 July 2025.
[96] Ibid.
[97] See character.ai: https://character.ai/ accessed 16 April 2024.
[98] Ibid: see the handles @Kapps98 and @elonwhisperer respectively for the relevant Sherlock Holmes and Elon Musk chatbots.

with these programs, and also show that there is a clear interest in individuals communicating with what (at least superficially) appears to be a real, well-known and living person rather than a fictional character. Academics have argued that advancements such as these in AI have led to online life and 'normal life' merging into an 'onlife'.[99] This onlife can increasingly lead to reputationally damaging disclosures of personal information online, as social interaction on the web is the new norm.

Another disturbing advancement powered by AI is the 'deepfake'. Deepfakes are pictures or videos that resemble a real-life individual to such an extent they could be mistaken for them. The developer of the deepfake has control over what is said or done by that likeness of a particular individual. Deepfakes now have the potential to be so convincing that it is extremely difficult to assess whether they are in fact fake, or instead real footage of a person – the developer quite literally can 'put new words into a politician's mouth'.[100] The technology works by running a large amount of pictures of the individual chosen to be impersonated through an AI algorithm, until a convincing image or video of that person can be created and manipulated.[101] The 'synthetic image' is then placed within a set of real images and the result will eventually resemble the person mimicked.[102] Powerful home desktops can now make deepfakes and easily accessible technology that can aid the process is now being developed.[103] As time progresses and AI becomes more

---

[99] Szocik and Jurkowska-Gomułka (n 92) 2, quoting Luciano Floridi, 'Soft ethics, the governance of the digital and the General Data Protection Regulation' (2008) 376(2133) *Philosophical Transactions of the Royal Society A: Mathematical, Physical and Engineering Sciences* 20180081.

[100] Ian Sample, 'What are deepfakes – and how can you spot them?' *The Guardian* (13 January 2020) www.theguardian.com/technology/2020/jan/13/what-are-deepfakes-and-how-can-you-spot-them accessed 4 December 2023.

[101] Ibid.

[102] Ibid.

[103] Ibid.

sophisticated – the more humans feed information to AI, the faster and more accurately it learns – the more difficult it will be to discern which videos or images are real and which fake. The use of AI to impersonate one's image, likeness or voice to commit crime has surged, due to the ever-increasing capabilities of AI making deepfake images and videos more convincing and difficult to determine.[104] Although software exists to help detect deepfakes, many people will not have ready access to such a program and instead rely on other subtle 'tells' with convincing videos, such as strange blinking patterns.[105] The difficulty in recognizing a well-produced deepfake is so significant that MIT launched a 'Detect Fakes' research project and accompanying website in order to train web users to recognize one.[106] The potential for deepfakes to spread false information about individuals is unparalleled. Deepfakes have been used so far to target two particular groups; to defame politicians and women,[107] with the rise of deepfake pornography.[108]

vi. Artificial intelligence and threats to reputation

As will be obvious from the discussion thus far, the most significant reputational threat that AI poses to individuals is the ability to accurately impersonate them. A deepfake

---

[104] Ben Colman, 'Why detecting dangerous AI is key to keeping trust alive in the deepfake era' (*World Economic Forum*, 7 July 2025) https://www.weforum.org/stories/2025/07/why-detecting-dangerous-ai-is-key-to-keeping-trust-alive/ accessed 24 July 2025.

[105] Sample (n 100).

[106] 'Detect DeepFakes: How to counteract misinformation created by AI' (*MIT Media Lab*) www.media.mit.edu/projects/detect-fakes/overview/ accessed 6 December 2024.

[107] See, for example, Jessica Ice, 'Defamatory political deepfakes and the First Amendment' (2019) 70(2) *Case Western Reserve Law Review* 417.

[108] See, for example, Anne Pechenik Gieseke, ' "The new weapon of choice": Law's current inability to properly address deepfake pornography' (2020) 73(5) *Vanderbilt Law Review* 1479.

video or a picture can be manipulated to do, say or show anything, which results in a range of potentially defamatory implications for the individual impersonated. While some deepfake hoax images are clearly satirical, others may not be; or may tread the line so closely it is difficult to tell. Combined with increasingly powerful software and hardware that can generate accurate likenesses, it is easy to see how deepfake content of a real individual engaged in reputational harmful activity could 'go viral' and receive multitudes of views online, engendering serious harm to one's reputation. Even after a successful defamation action is litigated, if such a video was seen by a significant section of the population this damage to reputation is incredibly difficult, if not impossible, to recover from. Although deepfakes have predominantly been used (in high-profile cases) to target public figures,[109] a user could also target a private individual who had incurred their ire if they had access to a suitable photoset and the requisite software and hardware.

Another clear reputational issue raised by AI advancements is if chatbot likenesses say or express views that are potentially defamatory to the 'real' individual mimicked. In addition to this eventuality, if a certain chatbot's algorithm (powered by machine learning) learns to engage in certain types of discussions or behaviour – such as sexist views or a proclivity to engage in sexually explicit or even flirtatious discussions with the user – this could lead to a latent belief in the public that the real-life individual on which a bot is based harbours those same proclivities, leading to potentially defamatory implications or innuendo. There is also the less fanciful possibility that a

---

[109] Particularly political figures or other public figures of note. This is clearly a widespread concern: see the University of Oxford's Reuters Institute of Journalism, which provided information about how to detect deepfake images in anticipation of the US and UK 2024 elections: https://reutersinstitute.politics.ox.ac.uk/news/spotting-deepfakes-year-elections-how-ai-detection-tools-work-and-where-they-fail accessed 26 August 2024.

text-based AI tool (such as Google's 'Gemini' – a chatbot which Google claims can 'supercharge your ideas')[110] generates results after a text prompt which contains defamatory information about a third party, and in effect publishes these to the human chat recipient or user. Widespread use of AI tools is still largely in its infancy and many users attest to repeated inaccuracies of results generated from text prompts or questions.[111] For example, if one uses an AI tool in order to search for a particular peer-reviewed article on a certain subject, an AI tool may boldly claim one exists and provide a citation – which is entirely false.[112] Many believe this is because, through machine learning, AI tools develop a bias to appear functional to a user and to 'please' by providing a result even when one does not exist. The reputational implications of an AI tool giving the false impression that a real individual has said, done or written something they have not are obvious.

Conclusion for Chapter 1

This chapter has argued that contemporary technological advancements have shaped and changed society such that increased threats to reputation are now widespread. Two types of advancement have been discussed: advancements that are, on the one hand, general and societal and, on the other, advancements of specific technologies presenting new threats to dignity. General developments (that impact not just the UK but

---

[110] See https://gemini.google.com/?hl=en accessed 26 August 2024.

[111] Readers can easily try this themselves by engaging with an AI tool and prompting it to tell them which article was written by person X on subject Y. What can be found is that, on occasion, the AI tool will entirely fabricate results. It also presents these results 'confidently' – see Thomas Lee, Daniel Campbell, Abhinav Rao, Afif Hossain, Omar Elkattawy, Navid Radfar, Paul Lee and Julius Gardin, 'Evaluating ChatGPT responses on atrial fibrillation for patient education' (2024) 16(6) *Cureus* e61680.

[112] Ibid.

many populations throughout the world) include the birth of social media and the increasing prevalence of internet-enabled devices. As handheld technology becomes more affordable, it also becomes increasingly commonplace in society and therefore more frequently used and ingrained into daily ways of life. This in turn changes patterns of human behaviour. Wider engagement with the internet in professional and private lives leads to the increasing likelihood that someone may upload potentially defamatory information about another to the web, as disclosures online are normalized. The advent of social media in the early 2000s shows no signs of stopping; although the *type* of social media site has altered in popularity,[113] engagement with social media continues to thrive. Posting personal and (potentially) defamatory information about another using a social media website is a convenient dissemination tool, able to be accessed more readily than print newspapers. There is now the additional concern of posts 'going viral' and amassing millions of views, and further difficulties of removing the online information that are not faced in the same way by purely print publications. The other type of advancement that this chapter has evaluated is the purely technological. Cloud computing powers websites and makes social media possible, storing vast data sets virtually – accessed using log-in credentials from anywhere. Virtual worlds, augmented reality and AI present unique threats to reputation. Virtual worlds can allow individuals to hide behind avatars but engage with other real people, and use a virtual world system to defame others by using voice or text. Augmented reality disrupts what we understand to be 'real' or 'fake' and can use false images overlaid onto real-life backgrounds to distort reality and engender a defamatory meaning. Advancements in AI can lead to a wide range of defamatory implications: chatbots could give misleading impressions about individuals they represent and

---

[113] Websites such as Snapchat or TikTok.

disclose false and damaging personal information about others (or their users), deepfakes can be used to spread likenesses of real people engaged in reputationally damaging activities, and AI tools can create and spread false personal information via their search results.

TWO

Searching for a Theoretical Basis of Defamation Law

Introduction

The previous chapter explored the extent of the problem: the sheer level of technological advancement the world has experienced and the increased potential threats towards reputation this poses. The aim of this chapter is to find a working, theoretical basis for the protections offered by English defamation law. Later chapters conduct an assessment of defamation law in the digital age and offer suggestions for legal improvements. One cannot move forward onto this more specific type of analysis before the reasons and theory behind legal protections extended by the law of defamation are examined. Finding a unified approach to the theory behind the ancient tort of defamation is not easy. In order to strike the heart of what defamation law is about, one must consider what it protects: reputation. Over centuries, there have been many theories espoused by lawyers, philosophers and sociologists that attempt to underpin legal protection for reputation. Part I of this chapter considers prominent theories behind the protection for reputation and advances a modern theoretical approach that forms this book's basis for both defining and protecting reputational interests. In so doing it will also evaluate more antiquated theoretical considerations behind reputation that have since been (at least partially) discredited by later scholarship and philosophical thought. After this jurisprudential basis has been established, Part II of the chapter considers a further element of this book's methodology. It sets out a range of named '*data-dissemination* scenarios' whereby personal, false and defamatory information is deposited on the internet. These scenarios form the medium of assessment for this monograph's subsequent analysis of the inadequate state of defamation law in light of technological change.

Defamation law is one of the most ancient laws, and torts, that currently exists in the English jurisdiction. In the Middle Ages, both spiritual and secular 'authorities' protected reputation.[1] Edward I's reign was the first time a solely secular jurisdiction dealt with defamation, taking it away, in large part, from the Ecclesiastical Courts.[2] After the King's Courts, the Star Chamber had unrestrained power and imported the Roman laws of *injuria* and *libellus famosus*, two criminal offences, to curtail the press after the Westminster Printing Press was established in 1476.[3] Much like the introduction of this printing press in the 15th century, another pivotal change has now occurred; the meteoric rise of the internet and internet-enabled technologies since the mid-2000s have heralded new potential for the wide dissemination of defamatory information. This book seeks to inspire a renaissance of defamation law, which it argues must adapt to overcome new and increasing threats to reputation posed by sophisticated technology. But first, this book now turns to the theory behind the importance of protecting reputational interests.

★★★

---

[1] Van Vechten Veeder, 'The history and theory of the law of defamation I' (1903) 3(8) *Columbia Law Review* 33, 546, 547.
[2] Ibid 551.
[3] Ibid 561–3.

Part I: The theory

Despite the vast number of words written and cases decided concerning defamation, judges and academics do not often stop to consider the *purpose* of defamation law in requisite detail. Writing comprehensively in the early 1900s, Van Veeder tells us that 'defamation professes to protect personal character and public institutions from destructive attacks, without sacrificing freedom of thought and the benefit of public discussion',[4] which can only partially now be said to be true in the English jurisdiction since public bodies cannot claim in defamation.[5] Others add that the law is based on 'damage to reputation, humiliation and exposure to public ridicule'[6] – and regardless of whether one is telling the truth when they publicly refute a defamatory claim, it is extremely difficult to stop a lie, even if one denies it.[7] Therefore, defamation law plays a role in publicly exonerating and vindicating a claimant as well as punishing a defamer. Whether one can in fact adequately restore a damaged reputation, even after public exoneration by the courts, is more doubtful. One thing that unites both law and literature in this area is the agreement that defamation law, at the very least, attempts to protect reputation. This book espouses a working theory behind defamation law: that it *acts to protect reputation and its impact upon personal dignity, perception of oneself and social life*. The aspects underlying this working theory (dignity, self-perception and social life) will now be examined in turn.

---

[4] Ibid 546.
[5] *Derbyshire County Council v Times Newspapers and Others* [1993] HL 18 Feb 1993.
[6] Jerome Neu, *Sticks and Stones: The Philosophy of Insults* (OUP 2008) 172.
[7] Ibid 173.

I. 'Dignity' as justifying defamation law

Dignity has been famously referred to by the US Supreme Court, as well as by certain members of the Strasbourg Court,[8] as the reason behind the legal protection of reputation.[9] Dignity was once an idea or concept that was limited to the upper class, but has over time permeated into all parts of society.[10] It is currently the most pervasive and persuasive explanation for what is protected when 'reputation' finds itself shielded by the law, although the term is both ephemeral and complex, as will be discussed.

a. The history of dignity

Fleming argues that dignity is 'the quality of being worthy or honourable; worthiness, worth'.[11] Historically, the concept has a wide range of potential sources. It has roots in revolutionary rhetoric, the work of Emmanuel Kant, Christianity and the words of Cicero.[12] Firstly, discussion of dignity can be traced back to the Bible's Old Testament.[13] Kant is credited with

---

[8] *Chauvy v France* App no 64915/01 (ECHR, 29 June 2004) 23; *Lindon v France* App nos 21279/02 and 36448/02 (22 October 2007) 39 and 40. See Tanya Alpin and Jason Bosland, 'The uncertain landscape of Article 8 of the ECHR: The protection of reputation as a fundamental human right?' in Andrew Kenyon (ed), *Comparative Defamation and Privacy Law* (CUP 2016) 276.

[9] Robert Post, 'The social foundations of defamation law: Reputation and the constitution' (1986) 74(3) *California Law Review* 69, 708.

[10] Ibid 716, and see Norbert Elias, *Power and Civility* (Edmund Jephcott, trans, Pantheon Books 1982) 309.

[11] John Fleming, *The Law of Torts* (8th edn, Law Book Company 1992), as highlighted by Professor Richard Mullender, Newcastle University, in 2013.

[12] Remy Debes, 'Dignity', *Stanford Encyclopedia of Philosophy* (18 February 2023) Part 1.2.1 https://plato.stanford.edu/entries/dignity/ accessed 29 July 2024.

[13] See Genesis 49:3, Esther 6:3, Ecclesiastes 10:6 and Habakkuk 1:7 in the King James Bible. The general concept of dignity could also be argued

popularizing a modern view of dignity, arguing that everyone is entitled to a 'kind of moral respect',[14] although Kant's thinking was in turn inspired by Rosseau and Samuel von Pufendorf.[15] There is also a moral concept of dignity, which emerges from Christianity – although there are arguments that the Christian concept does not clearly align with the modern view of dignity as constituting an inherent right of all humans.[16] Classical orator Cicero is thought to have had an unusually modern view of dignity; however, if his words are closely examined he does not clearly argue that dignity should engender basic human rights in order to protect it.[17] It is clear, then, that one universal historical 'origin story' cannot be found to ground the concept. Rather, the modern notion of dignity is perhaps an amalgamation of all the thinking described, subject to a wide range of influences and backgrounds.

b. Conceptualizing dignity

Due to the wide range of different meanings of the term dignity and different philosophical attitudes towards what it encompasses, many have argued that the term is now meaningless,[18] which is an unhelpfully pessimistic analysis.

---

   to be present in Jesus' teachings in the New Testament. With thanks to the Rev. Hugh Burgess for discussions on this point.

[14] Debes (n 12); and see Immanuel Kant, 'Groundwork of the metaphysics of morals (1785)', in Mary J Gregor (ed), *Practical Philosophy* (The Cambridge Edition of the Works of Immanuel Kant) (CUP 1996).

[15] Ibid Debes (n 12); and see Frederick C. Beiser, 'Kant's intellectual development: 1746–1781', in Paul Guyer (ed), *The Cambridge Companion to Kant* (CUP 1992) and Stephen Darwall, 'Pufendorf on morality, sociability, and moral powers' (2012) 50(2) *Journal of the History of Philosophy* 213 and 'Equal dignity and rights' in Remy Debes (ed), *Dignity: A History* (OUP 2017).

[16] Bonnie Kent, 'In the image of God: Human dignity after the fall' in Debes (n 15).

[17] Darwall (n 15).

[18] Debes (n 12).

Kolani has espoused that the term instead 'reflects something of "the beautiful"',[19] however unspecific this may be. Dignity may in fact be closer to a metaphorical term that represents what is at stake when another infringes someone's right to construct their own image. Attitudes towards dignity also differ around the globe. Strębska observes that Eastern and Western cultures diverge; the East adopts a 'face culture' concerned with traditional values (and external perceptions of how someone views another) and the West a 'dignity culture', more entwined with allowing individuals to choose how to represent themselves.[20] Indeed, one of the arguments in favour of the Western protection of personality interests such as privacy and reputation is on the grounds of individual autonomy, crucial to allowing individuals to present particular versions of themselves in public, by only disclosing personal information they so choose. Strębska's observations show that dignity is therefore capable of being seen as both a private right and a public issue.[21] There has to be, then, a relationship between the private and the public self, as Cooley and Mead have argued.[22] If there is a relationship between the private and the public self, it follows that there must also be a relationship between reputation as protecting both private and public welfare. Howarth notes that when discussing defamation reform, the Ministry of Justice made the mistake of viewing reputation as only impacting 'individual welfare', which clearly does not align with statements from the judiciary in cases such

---

[19] Ibid and Aurel Kolani, 'Dignity' (1976) 51(197) *Philosophy* 251.

[20] Katarzyna Strębska, 'Aging wars with words: Libel and slander in the Polish statutory law and English common law' (2014) 38(51) *Studies in Logic, Grammar and Rhetoric* 197, 205.

[21] Ibid 206.

[22] Post (n 9) 708, and see Charles Cooley, *The Two Major Works of Charles H. Cooley: Social Organization, Human Nature and the Social Order* (Free Press 1956) and George Herbert Mead, *Mind, Self, and Society* (University of Chicago Press 1934).

as *Reynolds*, to the effect that reputation (and therefore the protection of dignity) is inherent to the public interest and public good, affecting society more generally if it is allowed to be infringed.[23]

One thing that many philosophers agree on is that dignity has a connection to certain basic rights.[24] Dignity can be used positively to 'protect what has dignity'.[25] Waldron has observed that although theory may tell us that everyone is entitled to personal dignity, not everyone will find their dignity upheld – which is why the word is used to argue that the right should find protection in practice.[26] Dignity's 'home', he argues, should therefore be in the law.[27] One place where dignity is both clearly represented and protected is through the protection of reputation in defamation law.

c. Issues with dignity

i. Definitional difficulties

There are at the very least four definitions of dignity from the perspective of philosophy: dignity as manners, dignity as living up to certain modes of conduct, dignity as social status, and dignity as something that everyone has inherently and everyone must share.[28] Despite these differing viewpoints,

---

[23] David Howarth, 'Libel: Its purpose and reform' (2011) 74(6) *Modern Law Review* 845, 847.

[24] Debes (n 12) and see Teresa Iglesias, 'Bedrock truth and the dignity of the individual' (2001) 4(1) *Logos: A Journal of Catholic Thought and Culture* 114 and Doron Shultziner, 'Human dignity: Functions and meanings', in Jeff Malpas and Norelle Lickiss (eds), *Perspectives on Human Dignity: A Conversation* (Springer 2007) 73.

[25] Ibid Debes (n 12) and also in 'Dignity's gauntlet' (2009) 23 *Philosophical Perspectives* 45, 61–2.

[26] Ibid Debes (n 12) and Jeremy Waldron, 'Dignity, rank, and rights', in Meir Dan-Cohen (ed), *Berkeley Tanner Lecture* (OUP 2012).

[27] Ibid.

[28] Ibid Debes (n 12) Part 2.

some philosophical work has been undertaken to find common ground. A theory advanced by Killmister has merit as a unification of many different philosophical definitions of dignity; while it may not be easy for academics to agree on one *positive* definition of dignity, it is easier to find agreement when dignity has been violated.[29] Dignity is therefore harmonized through shared understandings of when it is infringed,[30] as it is a particular type of wrong which is 'normatively distinctive'.[31] To respect someone is intrinsically about human dignity – it is the 'operative fact' behind why we do so – and individuals are entitled to dignity as they have rational autonomy and souls.[32]

There are other legitimate critiques of dignity on a definitional basis. Rosen and McCrudden have argued that the concept is vacuous – the concept is not necessary to explain the law and the word is instead a 'placeholder' for other ideological 'battles' which are being fought.[33] There is indeed an ideological war being waged under the auspices of dignity as far as the protection of reputation and defamation law is concerned. The unrelenting struggle is between reputational control on the one hand, and unbridled freedom of expression on the other. But, unlike the views of Rosen and McCrudden, it is argued here that there is clear value in examining the theoretical rationale that underpins reputation, as this will help navigate the thin line that must be drawn between reputation's

---

[29] Ibid Debes (n 12) and Suzy Killmister, *Contours of Dignity* (OUP 2020).

[30] Ibid Debes (n 12).

[31] Ibid Debes (n 12) and Adam Etinson, 'What's so special about human dignity?' (2020) 48(4) *Philosophy & Public Affairs* 353, 357.

[32] Ibid Debes (n 12) and several texts by Stephen Darwall: 'Two kinds of respect' (1977) 88(1) *Ethics* 36; 'Respect as honour and accountability', in Stephen Darwall, *Honour, History and Relationship: Essays in Second-Personal Ethics II* (OUP 2013); and 'Equal dignity and rights', in Debes (n 15) 181.

[33] Ibid Debes (n 12) and Michael Rosen, *Dignity: Its History and Meaning* (Harvard University Press 2012) 149 and Christopher McCrudden, *Understanding Human Dignity* (OUP 2013), ch 1.

protection and expression in 'hard' cases. In terms of legal theory, Gearty has argued that the ambiguity of dignity can mean that it is 'easily abused' in courtrooms and in works on theoretical rights.[34] This is undoubtedly sometimes the case; it will be argued later in this book that the Defamation Act 2013, in its concerted prioritization of freedom of expression, failed to give reputation and therefore dignity sufficient credit and protection under the law.

ii. Dignity and balancing rights

Dignity cannot be universally protected by any aspect of the law. This is the case if, for example, another competing right is weighed against it – most obviously freedom of expression. Scott and Mullis have noted that a central problem with the balancing exercise between Article 8 ECHR and Article 10 rights is that it implies there is an objectively correct outcome, which they contend is not the case; both rights are mutually exclusive and judges will forever be criticized for how a case is decided when there is room for argument.[35] Many academics have criticized the ad hoc balancing of reputation – dignity values – and speech.[36] Descheemaeker has observed that the English courts' obligations to observe both ECHR rights and Strasbourg case law under the Human Rights Act has caused difficulties for this balancing act.[37] Despite these sincere

---

[34] Ibid Debes (n 12) and see Conor Gearty, 'The state of human rights' (2014) 5(4) *Global Policy* 391.

[35] Alistair Mullis and Andrew Scott, 'The swing of the pendulum: Reputation, expression and the recentering of English libel law' (2012) 61(3) *Northern Ireland Legal Quarterly* 27, 45.

[36] See, for example, Melville B Nimmer, 'The right to speak from times to time: First Amendment theory applied to libel and misapplied to privacy' (1968) 56(4) *California Law Review* 935.

[37] Eric Descheemaeker, 'Mapping defamation defences' (2015) 78(4) *Modern Law Review* 641, 648.

concerns, there is no clear alternative to the law engaging in some form of balancing exercise when competing rights of equal value conflict. There is also the question of whether dignity is engaged if a defamatory remark fails to damage an individual's psychological integrity. Using Mullis and Scott's argument, this should not engage Article 8 protection and dignity would fail to be protected, despite the fact that it could be negatively impacted.[38] This aligns with the viewpoint of the European Court of Human Rights (ECtHR), the court famously stating in *Karako* that harm to Article 8 interests is harm to 'psychological integrity' and only when libel is 'sufficiently serious' does it culminate in damaging such integrity.[39] This is problematic, as it introduces a threshold of seriousness before defamation can engage Article 8 interests. But both this threshold itself, as well as its measurement, are conceptually problematic. There is no clear dividing line when personal information becomes public or remains private, or is reputationally damaging *enough* to warrant Article 8 protection.[40] In echoes of Gearty's earlier warning,[41] the Strasbourg Court held that dignity is only *partly* protected by ECtHR law. It is also important to note that dignity of communication is a two-way right; it concerns both the dignity of the person 'attacked' (perhaps reputationally) by the communication, but is also concerned with the dignity of the speaker in communicating a message and, as such, forms a basis for the protection of freedom of expression.[42] Finally,

---

[38] Mullis and Scott (n 35) 47.

[39] Ibid 40; see also *Karako v Hungary* App no 39311/05 (ECHR, 28 April 2009) [21]. Also see *A v Norway* App no 28070/06 (ECHR, 9 April 2009), which concurs on this point.

[40] On this, see Fiona Brimblecombe and Gavin Phillipson, 'Regaining digital privacy? The new "right to be forgotten" and online expression' (2018) 4(1) *Canadian Journal of Comparative and Contemporary Law* 1, 37.

[41] Gearty (n 34).

[42] Ronald Dworkin, *Freedom's Law* (OUP 1999), ch 8.

there is also some limited philosophical disagreement over whether dignity forms the basis of rights. Waldron does not exclusively agree with this viewpoint – he instead argues that dignity is not the normative basis of rights, but legal rights *do* act to protect human dignity.[43] Others have noted that the concept of dignity actually pre-dates rights, giving rise to a 'chicken and egg' scenario.[44] Despite the fact that dignity is the most all-encompassing and compelling explanation for why the law seeks to protect reputation, it is clearly not without flaws as a theoretical basis.

d. 'Rival' theories to reputation as dignity

This chapter has argued that the most convincing theoretical basis that can comprehensively be understood as underpinning reputation is dignity. However, in historical works on defamation theory, several other theoretical justifications have been posited to lie behind reputation. These other theories have now been at least partially discredited by subsequent philosophical and legal thought, but are nevertheless important to consider as they have influenced law making in defamation's more distant past.

i. Defamation law as protecting honour

The idea of defamation law as protecting one's honour can be found in a range of historical sources, such as the works of Shakespeare and the Bible.[45] This type of honour, Post argues, is one of occupying a particular position in society, a

---

[43] See Waldon (n 26).
[44] See Debes (n 12); Michael Meyer, 'Dignity, rights and self-control' (1989) 99(3) *Ethics* 520, 521; and Jack Donnelly, 'Human rights and human dignity: An analytic critique of non-Western conceptions of human rights' (1982) 76(2) *American Political Science Review* 303.
[45] Post (n 9) 699.

certain 'social role', and others acknowledging this and acting accordingly.[46] This view has historically influenced defamation law; in the distant past, defamation laws only applied to noblemen according to the *De Scandalis Magnatum*, which was designed to stop upset between 'the King and his people or the great men of the realm'.[47] Duelling was also seen as a remedy or a resolution to defamation, something the Star Chamber sought to stop.[48] This form of honour or status was not earned but inherited.[49] Despite these historical origins, there are several important deficiencies that negate honour as a sufficient theoretical basis for reputation. Firstly, damages or monetary compensation as a remedy for defamation do not align with honour as it is protected by the law. The loss of honour, one's good name – 'can scarcely be comprehended by pecuniary damages' as the 'laundry of honour is only bleached with blood'.[50] More importantly, this is an antiquated stance. Western society has been steadily moving away from rigid social hierarchies and people no longer duel to defend their reputation. Honour is not a ground concept in the same way as dignity; what honour is concealing is a specific type of social worth and self-worth.[51] Dignity is in fact at the root of both. Past case law also demonstrates that it was not just the ruling classes who were interested in protecting their reputation; 'ordinary people' would also bring cases if they felt their honour was in jeopardy.[52] This is a trend that has very much continued into 2025 – although there have been many high-profile celebrity cases in defamation, one of the most well-known modern Supreme Court decisions on defamation

---

[46] Ibid 700.
[47] See Veeder (n 1) 554 and the document at 1,275.
[48] Veeder (n 1) 555.
[49] Post (n 9) 705.
[50] Ibid 703 and 705 respectively.
[51] Laurence McNamara, *Reputation and Defamation* (OUP 2007) 48.
[52] Ibid.

in the digital age, *Stocker v Stocker*, concerns a purely private couple and Facebook.[53] In fact, none of the three most recent Supreme Court defamation decisions concern high-profile claimants.[54] Defamation law is as valuable to purely private individuals today as it was ever.

ii. Personality rights as property

Another even earlier theory that was suggested as forming the basis for defamation law's protections was the idea of personality rights as proprietary rights. Post has observed that defamation at common law shows aspects of both the viewpoint of reputation as a market good – or property – and reputation as dignity.[55] Academics have argued that reputation and property are closely aligned, reputation akin to a tangible 'asset', if a 'peculiar one'.[56] This notion was widely popularized by Pound's article in the *Harvard Law Review* in 1915,[57] which suggests reputation is 'incorporeal property'.[58] The theory of personality rights as property rests on the idea that reputation can help individuals in the labour market.[59] This theory argues that someone can earn their reputation through talent and skill.[60] A real-life situation that aptly illustrates this particular claim were the lives of Roman merchants, an underclass who could, nevertheless, through hard work, earn a good living in Roman society. Sancinito explains:

---

[53] *Stocker v Stocker* [2019] UKSC 17.
[54] The other two being *Lachaux v Independent Print* [2019] UKSC 27 and *Serafin v Malkiewicz* [2020] UKSC 23.
[55] Post (n 9) 717.
[56] McNamara (n 51) 39.
[57] Roscoe Pound, 'Interests of personality' (1915) 28(4) *Harvard Law Review* 343, 349.
[58] Ibid 349. Pound in turn took inspiration from seminal work of Herbert Spencer, *Justice* (Williams and Norgate 1891).
[59] Post (n 9) 693.
[60] Ibid 694.

One's claim on that position was not something that could be relied upon to be stable or permanent, but, with sufficient work and luck, a merchant might achieve a good reputation, and once acquired and properly maintained, that reputation could be used to overcome the stigma against merchants, to reduce an individual's transaction costs, and to smooth the way to a successful career.[61]

This theory expounds that damaging someone's reputation can engender monetary loss,[62] which explains defamation law's role in protecting reputation – as good character equals creditworthiness.[63] McNamara observes that this idea is rooted in the idea of liberalism in 18th-century philosophy and the market society.[64]

There are several glaring problems with this theoretical position. Firstly, while this theory was at one time given credence by case law as underpinning defamation law, in recent history judges have moved away from crediting it as justifying reputational interests, instead now favouring language grounded in human dignity and human rights.[65] The property theory also fails to explain a great deal of the quirks of common law defamation, such as why harm or damage were automatically presumed for libel.[66] The theory also fails to explain why, for

---

[61] Jane Sancinito, *The Reputation of the Roman Merchant* (University of Michigan Press 2024) 8.
[62] Post (n 9) 694.
[63] Ibid 695.
[64] McNamara (n 51) 41.
[65] Ibid 40 and Post (n 9) 717 and 721. See, by way of example, Lord Wilson in *Serafin*. He discussed ECHR principles and ECtHR cases in the course of his assessment of the s 4 defence and the decisions of lower courts: *Serafin v Malkiewicz* [2020] UKSC 23 at [60] and [74].
[66] Post (n 9) 697–9. Note this position has subsequently changed as both slander and libel now must meet the serious harm threshold in s 1 Defamation Act 2013.

example, the s 1 serious harm threshold in the Defamation Act can implicitly be met without proof of economic loss for cases concerning private individuals; and in fact the point is often not argued at all and rather the threshold is assumed to be met with certain types of defamatory statements.[67] Most importantly, the property theory does not explain what is accurately lost from one's intrinsic being when someone has been defamed, publicly shamed or when damaging personal information concerning them has been posted online. It does not acknowledge that dignity is an inherent human right and that everyone has the right to have their dignity protected. Instead, the 'reputation as property' theory reduces the protection of reputation from the *human and the essential* to purely being a way to protect certain types of monetary interests.

II. The looking-glass self theory

The previous section has argued that dignity is the theory that most adequately explains what reputation is protecting through defamation law. However, this is not the end of the story. There are two other related *sub-theories* that are annexed to dignity and which illuminate, in a more specific way, certain aspects of the dignity theory and precisely what reputation is guarding against. The first of these sub-theories is the idea of the 'looking-glass self'. This notion argues that the perception of others fundamentally effects one's psychological perception of oneself.[68] The idea is that your identity is constructed not just by yourself but by other third-party individuals as well – and how they view you.[69] Howarth has argued that our perception of ourselves is in part based on the perceptions of others.[70] This is relevant in the Polish legal system, as 'integrity'

---

[67] See Chapter 3.
[68] Mullis and Scott (n 35) 41.
[69] Post (n 9) 709.
[70] Howarth (n 23) 854.

extends to the image that a person has of themselves, as well as how others perceive them.[71]

The looking-glass self theory originates from the works of Cooley and the idea is that it is the perception of our esteem in the eyes of others that in turn influences what we think about ourselves.[72] Socrates argued that the 'nobler' someone is, the more enraged they will be if treated unfairly – and Mullender has observed that this point applies 'not just to self-esteem, but to reputation'.[73] Therefore, there is a strong connection between reputation, self-esteem and, ultimately, dignity. Despite this, English law has not always accorded with this viewpoint. Strębska has argued that English law is more concerned with how the person reading the defamatory statement feels, rather than a claimant.[74] This is still – partially – true. In the recent case of *Dyson v Channel 4* that considered the requirement of reference to the claimant, the Court of Appeal stated that when an irrefutably clear reference is not obviously made, a court may need to consider the statement itself and the 'attributes of a claimant known to the hypothetical acquaintance' (or reader).[75] A great deal of importance is therefore attached to what a reader (or audience member) thinks, knows or feels – rather than a claimant. However, there have been other recent changes to the law which cast doubt on Strębska's rather blanket statement. In assessing whether the serious harm threshold has been met, the Supreme Court

---

[71] Strębska (n 20) 207.
[72] Alpin and Bosland (n 8) 270.
[73] Plato, *Republic* (440c–d). This point was made by Professor Richard Mullender, Newcastle University Law School, in 2013, and the direct quotation is from his lecture.
[74] Strębska (n 20) 207.
[75] [2023] EWCA Civ 884 and Helena Shipman, 'Case law: *Dyson v Channel 4*, Court of Appeal grants claimants' appeal on reference' (*Inforrm's Media Law Blog*, 29 July 2023) https://inforrm.org/2023/07/29/case-law-dyson-v-channel-4-court-of-appeal-grants-claimants-appeal-on-reference-helena-shipman/ accessed 31 July 2024.

in *Lachaux* explained that a relevant consideration is *how many people that knew the claimant in the course of everyday life had seen the defamatory content* and therefore how much the claimant's life will be impacted – and in turn, how far will it affect how they feel about themselves.[76] Consequently, it seems that at least some recent interpretations at common law originate from the looking-glass self theory.

The theory also finds support in Strasbourg jurisprudence. In *Karako*, the ECtHR found that the protection of reputation is important because of the harm caused through a particular, negative view of a person being presented – and the ultimate effect on that person about how they feel about themselves.[77] Others, however, have argued that the decision in *Karako* also questions the looking-glass theory, as the ECtHR differentiated between *self-esteem* that is protected by reputation and capable of being damaged by 'external valuation' and *personal integrity*, which 'remains inalienable'.[78] The court found that statements or publications must be sufficiently serious 'as to undermine personal integrity'.[79] In this respect, the decision of the court is conceptually flawed, as it draws an arbitrary distinction between two things which are aspects of the same. A significant blow to one's self-esteem through reputational harm can engender damage to personal integrity itself, as this is surely influenced by self-worth. If the ECtHR felt it necessary to instate a threshold of severity, it would have been more prudent for the court to simply argue that to engage Article 8 rights, reputational infringements have to be sufficiently serious as to warrant the court's attention – as the ECtHR is not concerned with trifles.[80] Judge Jočinė

---

[76] *Lachaux* (n 54) [21].
[77] *Karako v Hungary* (n 39) and Mullis and Scott (n 35) 28.
[78] *Karako* (n 77) [22].
[79] Ibid.
[80] Which is the justification behind the s 1 threshold introduced in the Defamation Act 2013.

in the case also expressed concerns about this aspect of the majority decision in *Karako*, with the matter (in her learned opinion) requiring 'careful future consideration'.[81]

Howarth questions the simplicity of the looking-glass theory, arguing that an adult's perception of themselves is not a mirror image of what others think about them – and that a person would instead contest someone's opinion about them rather than blindly accept it.[82] This is undoubtedly true, as the looking-glass self theory only describes one narrow aspect of what can be protected against by defamation law – and does not necessarily reflect the whole measure of how someone feels about themselves, which is influenced by a myriad of internal and external factors. This is why the looking-glass self theory can only be accepted as an explanation of a little part of what reputation rights protect against, itself a small annexed theory to the broader notion of *dignity* as what is fundamentally shielded by defamation law.

III. Defamation law as protecting human sociality and relationships

The second and final *sub-theory* of reputation as protecting dignity that needs to be examined is the idea that reputational protection strengthens human sociality and interpersonal relationships. Again, like the looking-glass self, this is a sub-theory which is related to the broader and more encompassing notion that reputation and therefore defamation law shield human dignity.

The sociality theory is famously argued by Post in his article in the early 1900s. Post believed that defamation law had two functions: 'rehabilitation of individual dignity and maintenance of communal identity'.[83] The notion is also supported by

---

[81] *Karako* (n 77) 'Partly Concurring Opinion of Judge Jočienė' [7].
[82] Howarth (n 23) 857.
[83] Post (n 9) 715.

philosophical works, such as that by Iglesias, who argues that dignity and the human rights that protect it shield not just *individual* dignity but also 'community relationships'.[84] Post explains that defamation law serves a function of 'an enforcement of society's interest in its rules of civility'.[85] Howarth concurs and argues that the idea of defamation as simply protecting individual dignity is unduly basic, as it fails to consider how it can also protect human relationships.[86] Modern literature concerning social media has also been inspired by the sociality theory as a theoretical basis; the 'importance of social networks to the formulation of reputations(s)' has been discussed by Craik.[87] The theory also holds true for civilizations in ancient history: when considering reputations of Roman merchants, Sancinito argues that reputation is 'a collaborative endeavour'.[88] It appears, then, that this theory has stood the test of time.

The idea that reputation strengthens community bonds has sociological roots. In sociology, community itself is a moral good; traditions are reinforced by participation in the community and those who do not comply are eventually removed from the fold.[89] Society also equals 'association' – participation in society makes life easier, in that it both connects and separates us from others.[90] Defamation law supports society as it protects certain social values that are deemed to have merit (at the time) and holds potentially defamatory statements to account against these values.[91] In this sense, the law must

---

[84] See Debes (n 12) and Iglesias (n 24) 130.
[85] Post (n 9) 711.
[86] Howarth (n 23) 853.
[87] Kenneth H. Craik, *Reputation: A Network Interpretation* (OUP 2009) and Sancinito (n 61) 14.
[88] Sancinito (n 61) 15.
[89] McNamara (n 51) 24 and Ferdinand Tönnies, *Gemeinschaft and Gesellschaft* (Fues's Verlag 1887).
[90] Tönnies (n 89) and McNamara (n 51) 24 and 25.
[91] Neu (n 6) 180.

be careful about what statements it considers defamatory, as finding that this is the case signals that these statements are undesirable,[92] and sends social and moral messages to society as a result. This reinforces some behaviours and condemns others. Reputation is also 'one of the key means through which humans defend cooperation'.[93] Physical (and mental) repercussions like shame and pride transform our behaviour when we have done (or experienced) something 'socially damaging or rewarding'.[94] Reputation has a contextually objective good in that it maintains certain types of social bonds and socialization.[95] This has been the case since the dawn of civilization: in the case of ancient Rome, 'fear of losing a good reputation, or developing a bad one, pressured merchants to avoid certain kinds of conduct, and encouraged them to behave in socially acceptable ways'.[96]

Beyond supporting community groups, academics have argued that *individual* personality also depends on 'general social perspectives'.[97] In other words, the internalization of social roles and third-party perspectives can also constitute individual identity. Post argues that individual identity is constituted through social interactions, as people live by certain rules in a social order.[98] As alluded to, the results of a bad reputation are social 'ostracism'.[99] Howarth notes that the negative effects of this should not be trivialized as there has been research that observes extreme human reactions to social ostracism, such as illness.[100] He argues that part of the reason defamation should

---

[92] Ibid.
[93] John Whitfield, 'The biology of reputation', in Hassan Masum and Mark Tovey (eds), *The Reputation Society* (MIT Press 2011) 40.
[94] Ibid.
[95] Howarth (n 23) 849.
[96] Sancinito (n 61) 9.
[97] Post (n 9) 708, and Mead (n 22).
[98] Post (n 9) 708 and 709.
[99] Howarth (n 23) 850.
[100] Ibid 852.

be actionable is the 'pain' caused by ostracism.[101] An individual's private life would undoubtedly be impacted by exclusion or impending exclusion from their social group.[102]

Defamation law as facilitating human relationships/sociality is a theory relied on in both English and Strasbourg case law. In *Guardian News and Media Ltd*, the Supreme Court observed that control against defamatory material facilitated personal relationships in society,[103] and considered how the claimant's interpersonal relationships and his relationships within the community would be affected.[104] Further, in *Pfeifer v Austria*, the Strasbourg Court considered that an individual's interactions with others fall under the auspices of Article 8 ECHR.[105] Strębska argues that in defamation cases how a person is perceived in the public eye is crucial.[106] This is, of course, directly concerned with 'face' and how lack of 'face' may impact external relationships. In terms of harm, Alpin and Bosland also observe that the sociality theory is focused on the physical and psychological damage of social ties being broken, which is different to self-esteem.[107] It is argued here that the looking-glass self theory is more concerned with self-esteem. Howarth argues in favour of the sociality sub-theory at the root of defamation law, distilling the purpose of the law into a few sentences: 'The most important lesson to be drawn is that defamation protects a fundamental human interest in sociality, an interest that is fully capable of justifying restraints on freedom of expression in many circumstances.'[108]

---

[101] Ibid.

[102] Alpin and Bosland (n 8) 272.

[103] Scott and Mullis (n 35) 41 and *Re Guardian News and Media Ltd* [2010] UKSC 1, [2010] 2 AC 697 [42] and [74].

[104] Ibid.

[105] Howarth (n 23) 857; *Pfeifer v Austria* App no 12556/03 (ECHR, 15 November 2007) [33].

[106] Strębska (n 20) 208.

[107] Alpin and Bosland (n 8) 272.

[108] Howarth (n 23) 864.

This sub-theory is, of course, broader than simply claiming that reputation protects individual relationships; it also argues that reputational protection protects human sociality *more generally*, and strengthens communities by reinforcing shared values and a sense of belonging, as Post has famously noted. Finally, before concluding, it is important to consider how defamatory statements can more specifically damage social ties.

a. Strong and weak ties

One of the reasons that robust defamation law is crucial for strong societies is because if an individual is falsely accused of something extremely serious, this can damage even 'strong ties' or previously robust social bonds; the impact of this on mental health can be catastrophic.[109] It is this sort of life-altering claim that engenders strong reputational protection from the law and this is still broadly the case even after the enactment of the Defamation Act 2013, which reduced reputational protection. A less serious defamatory claim may only break 'weak ties', perhaps rendering financial rather than social harm.[110] However, the importance of the protection of weak ties should also not be overlooked; financial harm is very much a real harm (indeed, the demonstration of 'serious financial loss' can prove the s 1(2) serious harm threshold for businesses is met). Loss of a livelihood can render families destitute. Social networks more broadly can also be lost in the rupturing of weak ties;[111] one can still be ostracized from the social group if a myriad of weak ties have been broken. Defamation law has often accorded with an assessment of how likely social ties are to be broken by a given statement – the more likely they are to be broken, the more likely a claim is held to be

---

[109] Ibid 856.
[110] Ibid.
[111] Ibid 857.

actionable. Neu has observed that in the French Press Law of 1881, defamation was determined on how severe the claim was – and therefore the more likely to damage ties – and not its truth.[112] Similarly, as will be discussed in the next chapter of this book, s 1 of the Defamation Act 2013 now obliges courts to consider whether a defamatory statement has rendered or is likely to render serious harm to a claimant's reputation.

To summarize this pervasive sub-theory, defamation law 'must imply confirmation of membership in that community' when 'interests in civility' have been violated.[113] The relationships/sociality theory supports the idea of dignity lying behind reputation, as dignity is restored if a court upholds a defamation claim and finds community norms have been breached.[114] A court in this instance is speaking for the community – the ruling confirms the claimant's right to be part of it and signals that they are worthy of respect.[115] Until jury trials were all but abolished by s 11 of the Defamation Act 2013, the community *was* directly speaking in defamation trials as a jury decided on the meaning of the words; a judge now instead decides, representing the social group at large.

IV. Concluding remarks for Part I

This chapter has argued that the most convincing, all-encompassing and prevalent theoretical justification behind the legal protection of reputation is dignity. Dignity as a definition is not without drawbacks; it is a wide notion, including personal dignity and dignity as it supports society and wider social groups. Despite being a broad concept born of many

---

[112] Neu (n 6) 172, 176.
[113] Post (n 9) 712.
[114] Ibid 713.
[115] Ibid 713.

different historical roots, philosophers have proved that the term is capable of definition – even if this is a negative one (it is clear when dignity rights have been violated).[116] As has been argued, a violation of dignity is both recognizable and distinctive in the law – and is therefore deserving of robust protection by the laws of defamation. The notion of defamation common law and statutes as protecting honour or property has had some historical influence over law making, but this chapter has argued that both concepts are redundant in the modern era. The idea of honour as defamation law's theoretical basis is outdated as it subscribes to a rigid class system which is no longer a feature of contemporary society. The concept of reputation as personal property was fundamentally legally flawed from the start – the idea of reputation as being solely something traded for profit does not adequately explain what is lost when reputation has been damaged. The smaller, more specific theories of reputation as protecting someone's view of themselves (the looking-glass self theory) and the idea of defamation law as protecting social relationships and society more generally are both also persuasive, and illustrate specific negative repercussions when reputation is harmfully infringed. Both ultimately collapse into the idea of personal dignity as the theoretical backbone that underpins reputation. The working theory that this book will proceed with, then, is that defamation law *acts to protect reputation and its impact upon personal dignity, perception of oneself and social life.* The following legal analysis that this book undertakes will conduct analysis from this theoretical standpoint.

★★★

---

[116] See Killmister (n 29).

Part II: The scenarios

In order to conduct the analysis that follows, this book will consider defamation law in the digital age not only using the discussed theoretical basis but also through a number of *data-dissemination* scenarios. These scenarios describe the various ways that personal, potentially defamatory content can find itself distributed on the internet. The way in which this information is deposited online has repercussions for claimants, in terms of how and against whom they can bring an action in defamation. It also has repercussions theoretically, as will be argued in this book, in terms of how the present law should be interpreted to best protect claimants who are increasingly being defamed online. The web is inherently complex, both practically and legally; these scenarios help in understanding both how the web works and the best routes for legal recourse when someone is defamed in this particular way. These defamation scenarios will also streamline analysis that will be undertaken when this book turns to the alternative course of action that an individual can undertake to remove defamatory personal data on the internet; the 'right to be forgotten', also known as the right to erasure in Article 17 of the UK GDPR. These dissemination scenarios are not exhaustive and discussion of legal eventualities will take place in this book outside of these categories; however, these scenarios are nonetheless significant as a methodology anchoring discussion of the most prevalent difficulties facing defamation law in the digital era.

The *data-dissemination* scenarios are such:

I. The defamation by social media *scenario*

Person Z uploads defamatory, personal information about person M to a social networking site that is accessible on the internet – powered by cloud-computing technology.

This could be to a more traditional social media site, such as Facebook or X/Twitter, or to a more modern version of such a site, like TikTok or Snapchat, which focuses on short-form video or photographic content rather than text. Legal questions arising from this scenario include how seriously defamatory content posted online rather than through traditional print media is considered at common law and whether content posted to social media in this way would likely satisfy the serious harm threshold as per s 1 of the Defamation Act 2013. A further question is the impact of 're-posting' defamatory content that has been spread on social media in this way, either in meeting the serious harm threshold or in terms of other routes to redress for claimants.

II. The third-party poster *scenario*

In this *data-dissemination* scenario, defamatory content has reached the internet through being posted by person P to website Q. The owners of the host website believe in upholding freedom of expression on the internet and do not have time to regularly monitor all of the comments uploaded to their website. This particular scenario would engage the s 5 defence for operators of host websites and the annexed regulations within the statutory instrument.[117] Broadly explained, if a claimant complains they have been defamed in the post of a third-party to website *host*, it is a defence for a website host to comply with the terms of the statutory instrument. The regulations stipulate that the host must contact the author of the post to request their identification details so action can be taken against them; if they refuse (or cannot be contacted), the post will be removed after

---

[117] See The Defamation (Operators of Websites) Regulations 2013, UK Statutory Instruments 2013 No 3028 www.legislation.gov.uk/uksi/2013/3028/schedule/made accessed 8 August 2024.

five days.[118] There are questions around how this defence will be interpreted by the courts in practice and whether it represents an appropriate balance between protecting the reputations of individuals and fostering freedom of speech on online platforms.

III. The defamation by AI tool or virtual world *scenario*

In this scenario, individual F is defamed by artificial intelligence (AI)-powered software and this defamatory content is then uploaded on the internet. There is a range of potentialities housed under this particular scenario. As AI gains provenance, it continues to be funded by large corporations and enhanced by further research to strengthen its machine-learning capabilities. The more developed AI tools become, the more likely convincing deepfakes can be easily constructed and then uploaded online in picture or video form to convey a defamatory meaning. Even in 2025, AI already presents a myriad of defamatory potentialities; as discussed in Chapter 1, the website character.ai hosts a range of chatbots, some bearing close resemblances to real people.[119] Chatbots could seemingly engage in conversations, powered entirely by machine learning, that could potentially render defamatory meanings. Augmented reality tools – which are even more prominent – could be used to create videos or images that could result in a defamatory innuendo by manipulating images against real-world backgrounds. Further, this scenario will also consider the possibility where person F is defamed by an avatar in a virtual world; the defamatory statement is communicated via voice or text in an online world to other living individuals, also inhabiting avatars (with access to the virtual world using a VR headset). Questions

---

[118] Ibid Schedule 2.
[119] See https://character.ai/ accessed 3 July 2025.

arise of jurisdiction, intention and who the appropriate defendant would be in such cases.

IV. The repetition of statements online over a year later scenario

In this scenario, person W publishes a defamatory statement *on the internet* that has previously been published over a year earlier. Section 8 of the Defamation Act 2013 abolished the common law rule of *Brunswick v Harmer*, that every republication of a defamatory statement gave rise to a fresh cause of action, as it engenders new reputational harm.[120] This long-standing common law rule worked in favour of those defamed, as it gave claimants a fresh route to redress if a defamatory statement about them was repeated, with its previous utterance long since forgotten. In abolishing the multiple publication rule, the new s 8 'single publication rule' states that time starts to run on the date of a defamatory statement's first publication – after a year has passed, it prohibits any further action taken against the republication of the defamatory statement *in substantially the same form* by the same publisher. How widely the concept of 'substantially the same form'[121] should be interpreted is ripe for consideration, in how it relates to the differences between posts first published in print and then appearing online or vice versa, and what exactly is meant by substantially the same form as far as posting on the internet is concerned (be it published on social media, the virtual world, collated by an AI tool or otherwise).

---

[120] *Duke of Brunswick v Harmer* [1950] 175 ER 441.
[121] There is some guidance in sections (4) and (5) of s 8 Defamation Act 2013, although these still require the courts to flesh them out through case law.

V. Concluding remarks for Part II

These scenarios will be discussed, along with other prevalent legal issues, in Chapter 3. The dissemination scenarios are forms of literary methodology and not intended to incorporate all of the discussions that this book will engage in concerning online defamation. Rather, they are touchstones of some of the most pressing online eventualities that must be addressed in order to help both academics and practitioners navigate the interpretation of defamation law in the digital world. The next chapter of this book will examine each of these scenarios in turn.

THREE

How Online Defamation Cases Are Decided

This chapter will rely on the *data-dissemination* scenarios outlined in Chapter 2 in order to guide its analysis into the difficulties potential claimants face in cases of online defamation. It is separated into two parts; Part I is primarily concerned with the impact of the Defamation Act 2013 and how this has negatively affected claimants in online defamation actions. In this sense, Part I focuses on *legal* changes and the challenges these pose to those defamed in various ways on the web. Part II of this chapter is concerned instead with *technological* changes, which have increased the prevalence of defamatory content online and altered the digital landscape, and the intersection of these changes with libel actions. The overarching theme of this chapter is an examination of how English defamation law and the judiciary have responded to the changing digital landscape and increasing defamatory content online. This chapter will argue that there is much more that needs to be done in order to reinstate reputational interests in an online context and that the law as it currently stands is failing claimants in a number of ways.

★★★

Part I: Difficulties for claimants posed by the Defamation Act 2013

This section will firstly consider the s 1 threshold of 'serious harm' as caused or likely to be caused by a particular statement required by the 2013 reform. This reform was introduced by the Act with the intention of making bringing an action in defamation by a claimant more difficult and therefore 'weeding out' what were considered by some to be weaker claims. As will be argued, s 1 has a potentially prohibitive impact on everyone who wishes to mount an action in defamation by raising the threshold to bring an action across the board – but may pose particular problems to those arguing that they have been defamed on the internet. This will invoke the *defamation by social media* scenario outlined in Chapter 2. Secondly, the introduction of a limitation period of one year for repetitions of defamatory statements introduced by s 8 of the Act will be considered. This replaced the long-standing rule in *Brunswick v Harmer*,[1] where every repetition of a defamatory statement gave rise to a fresh action in defamation, regardless of how much time had passed between this and the initial publication. It seems clear that this limitation period will also apply to defamatory statements posted on the internet – and invokes the *repetition of statements online over a year later* scenario, also outlined in Chapter 2.

Both of these changes introduced by the 2013 reform have 'swung' English defamation law in favour of freedom of expression, at the expense of the protection of individual reputation and therefore personal dignity. These legal changes and both defamation scenarios will be examined in the context of defamation through the mode of the internet.

---

[1] *Duke of Brunswick v Harmer* [1950] 175 ER 441: the traditional rule was that every republication of a defamatory statement gives rise to a new claim.

I. Online publication and the 'serious harm' threshold

a. Background to the reform

Libel reform in the Defamation Act 2013 could not have come at a worse time. As discussed in Chapter 1, the world is now in the grip of the digital age – with increased threats to individual reputation through defamation on the internet. Despite this, English and Welsh libel law was changed in 2013 in order to tilt legal precedent in favour of *expression* rather than the protection of individual reputation. One of the key ways this rebalancing was achieved through the 2013 Act was by raising the threshold a claimant must meet in order to bring an action in defamation, irrespective of whether the defamatory statement appears online or in print. This provides a further barrier to the protection of personal dignity through reputation rights in the face of the unbridled potential to defame using the internet. The purpose of the introduction of the 'serious harm threshold' in s 1 of the Defamation Act 2013 was to 'raise the bar' as to what type of statement could be actionable in defamation law, to include only those which have caused (or could likely cause) serious reputational harm to the claimant.[2] The idea behind this was that it would curtail potentially 'spurious' claims and strengthen freedom of expression generally. The High Court in *Courtney v Ronksley* explains the change in the law:

> Defamation is an abridgment of free speech. When it introduced the serious harm test, Parliament's intention was to allow a greater margin to free speech, and to prevent the scarce and precious public resources of the senior courts from being occupied with defamation challenges to others' freedom of expression, unless

---

[2] Section 1(1) Defamation Act 2013.

objectively demonstrable real-life reputational impact can be established, on ordinary causational grounds, and to a proper threshold of gravity.[3]

The 2013 reform was enacted because journalists, human rights campaigners, scientists and other pressure groups argued that their legitimate speech was being curtailed as a result of concerns about libel actions. As a result, it became an election promise on both sides of the House that English libel law would be reformed to reprioritize expression interests.[4] This was partly achieved by the introduction of the serious harm threshold in s 1. Sewell has argued that the introduction of s 1 (and its interpretation by courts) is a good thing, as it is 'inspiring parties to resolve their case away from court'.[5] The accuracy of this can be questioned; certainly, if one considers the number of high-profile celebrity defamation cases in the last five years this does not seem to be true – but the sentiment that this in fact would be a positive outcome regardless should also be challenged.[6] If there has been reputational damage arguably accrued on the basis of a defamatory statement (that

---

[3] *Courtney v Ronksley* [2024] EWHC 572 (KB) [64].

[4] Charlie Sewell, 'More serious harm than good? An empirical observation and analysis of the effects of the serious harm requirement in section 1(1) of the Defamation Act 2013' (2020) 12(1) *Journal of Media Law* 47, 50–1 and English PEN, 'Libel Reform Campaign' www.englishpen.org/campaign/uk-free-speech/libel-reform-campaign/ accessed 28 November 2024. Also see Andrew Scott, 'Impact case study: Reforming England's libel law' www.lse.ac.uk/Research/research-impact-case-studies/reforming-englands-libel-law#:~:text=He%20found%20that%20reform%20of,philosophy%20and%20human%20rights%20law accessed 28 November 2024.

[5] Sewell (n 4) 56.

[6] Such as *Vardy v Rooney* [2021] EWHC 1888 (QB); *Depp II v News Group Newspapers Ltd* [2020] EWHC 2911 (QB); and *Blake v Fox* [2023] EWCA Civ 1000.

cannot be shown to be true),[7] the correct method to rectify the damage to personal dignity caused is for claimants to 'have their day in court' and to have it proclaimed to the world in a legal decision that a defendant is liable for the statement. If claimants are dissuaded from pursuing potentially legitimate actions on the basis of s 1, this may in fact operate as a barrier to justice. Sewell argues that it will at the very least deter 'opportunistic claims',[8] although there is little evidence that this was a problem to begin with. To the contrary, with the ease, speed and worldwide reach of the internet it is now simple to disseminate defamatory information about another, particularly using social media websites (such as the case in the *defamation by social media* scenario).

Section 1 was introduced despite the fact that safeguards for freedom of expression had been present at common law for some time before the adoption of the Defamation Act 2013. The pre-existing case law of *Thornton* and *Jameel* dictated that a 'tendency'[9] to cause 'substantial' reputational harm was the threshold necessary to bring a claim,[10] a threshold articulated to account specifically for Article 10 European Convention on Human Rights (ECHR) concerns. Hyde has noted that spurious claims were therefore already able to be struck out

---

[7] According to s 2 Defamation Act 2013, now known as the truth defence (formerly justification) – substantial truth is the threshold required under s 2(1).

[8] Sewell (n 4) 57.

[9] See Iain Wilson and Tom Double, 'Business as usual? The Court of Appeal considers the threshold for bringing a libel claim in *Lachaux v Independent Print Ltd*' (*Inforrm's Blog*, 16 September 2017) https://inforrm.org/2017/09/16/business-as-usual-the-court-of-appeal-considers-the-threshold-for-bringing-a-libel-claim-in-lachaux-v-independent-print-ltd-iain-wilson-and-tom-double/ accessed 28 November 2024.

[10] *Thornton v Telegraph Media Group* [2010] EWHC 1414 (QB) [94] and *Jameel (Youssef) v Dow Jones & Co Inc* [2005] QB 946 [40] and [55].

under common law rules before s 1 was adopted, serving to raise this threshold higher still.[11]

b. Interpretive difficulties: what exactly is the new s 1 'serious harm' threshold?

For a claimant to bring an action in defamation in respect of a post on the internet (such as on Facebook) or otherwise, s 1(1) of the Defamation Act 2013 tells us that 'a statement is not defamatory unless its publication has caused or is likely to cause serious harm to the reputation of the claimant'.[12] In essence, this challenges a claimant's ability to prove they have an 'evidential basis' for their claim from the outset.[13] It also erodes the distinction between libel and slander – slander is traditionally only actionable with proof of special damage,[14] whereas libel was actionable per se because of its more permanent nature.[15] This distinction, as it applies to online posts (or statements more generally),[16] has therefore ceased to be important – the question now is, how precisely must one adduce whether a post on a website such as Facebook meets the s 1 threshold. Any requiem for the distinction between libel and slander should perhaps be none too hasty, as Van Veeder has observed the distinction was a result of a historical anachronism and difficult to reconcile with modern media such as the internet.[17]

---

[11] Richard Hyde, 'Procedural control and the proper balance between public and private interests in defamation claims' (2014) 6(1) *Journal of Media Law* 47, 66.

[12] Section 1(1) Defamation Act 2013.

[13] Hyde (n 11) 66.

[14] *Roberts v Roberts* [1864] 33 LJ QB 249.

[15] See, for example, *Monson v Tussauds Ltd* [1894] 1 QB 671.

[16] See *Tamiz v Google* [2013] EWCA Civ 68.

[17] Van Vechten Veeder, 'The history and theory of the law of defamation II' (1904) 4(1) *Columbia Law Review* 33, 54

Perhaps because of the rather thin explanation of the new threshold in s 1(1) of the Act, the question of what precisely the new test requires has been left to the courts,[18] and the idea of showing 'likelihood' of serious harm occurring has resulted in different interpretations.[19] The very early case of *Cooke* held that s 1 operated a higher standard than what was previously required at common law, although evidence will not always be required.[20] Similarly, another early case, *Ames*, held that s 1 had raised the threshold as previously existent at common law, although serious harm could be inferred without evidence of an adverse reaction from readers.[21] A few years later in 2017, in *Monroe v Hopkins*, part of the claimant's case with regards to what constituted serious harm in s 1(1) was that she had 'trouble sleeping' and was anxious about the backlash she could face on social media due to defamatory tweets about her, an argument accepted by Mr Justice Warby.[22] The learned judge went on to say that 'the serious harm requirement is satisfied, on the straightforward basis that the tweets complained of have a tendency to cause harm to this claimant's reputation in the eyes of third parties, of a kind that would be serious for her',[23] implying that the threshold is not only highly practical in nature, but also a somewhat subjective standard. Mr Justice Warby went on to observe that that if the statement is seriously defamatory and widely published, this may be enough to satisfy s 1 without any further evidence being adduced.[24]

After a number of years of uncertainty for claimants, the judgment of the Court of Appeal in *Lachaux* was delivered in 2017.[25] The Court of Appeal famously disagreed with the

---

[18] Sewell (n 4) 52.
[19] Ibid.
[20] *Cooke v MGN Ltd* [2014] EWHC 2831 (QB) [37] and [43] respectively.
[21] *Ames v Spamhaus Project Ltd* [2015] EWHC 127 (QB) [55].
[22] *Monroe v Hopkins* [2017] EWHC 433 (QB) [64].
[23] Ibid [70].
[24] Ibid [69].
[25] *Lachaux v Independent Print Ltd and Another* [2017] EWCA Civ 1334.

decision of (once again) Mr Justice Warby in the same matter at the High Court. The latter had argued previously that the bar had been raised from the common law position and that claimants must go further than merely showing the *tendency* to cause reputational harm. Judge Warby argued that it must be shown by evidence that serious harm to one's reputation had been caused, or was likely to be caused in the future.[26] The Court of Appeal did not adopt Judge Warby's reasoning – rather, they found that the threshold had merely been changed from that which was *substantial* to *serious*, with seriousness nevertheless being a more significant standard in terms of proof required to meet it.[27] The Court of Appeal found that Judge Warby's more radical interpretation, which was a more marked change from the position at common law, was not what parliament had intended.[28] Essentially, the position the Court of Appeal adopted in *Lachaux* was that of '*Thornton*-plus';[29] the threshold was raised from the position at common law, but raised only slightly. The decision was once again appealed, this time in the Supreme Court, where the debate about how high the bar had exactly been raised from the position at common law was firmly laid to rest. Lord Sumption delivered the judgment, rejecting the Court of Appeal's interpretation of s 1 in favour of Judge Warby's original decision at the High Court.[30] Lord Sumption held that 'actual facts' about the impact of the words are relevant to determining s 1 and it 'raises the threshold of seriousness' above that which existed in *Jameel* and *Thornton*.[31] Whether s 1 was met, Lord Sumption found, 'depends on a combination of the *inherent tendency* of the words and *their actual impact* on those to whom they were

---

[26] See Wilson and Double (n 9).
[27] Ibid. *Lachaux v Independent Print* (n 25) [56ff].
[28] *Lachaux v Independent Print* (n 25) [56]–[59].
[29] Sewell (n 4) 55.
[30] *Lachaux v Independent Print* [2019] UKSC 27 [20].
[31] Ibid [12].

communicated'.[32] The Supreme Court decision signalled a considerable change from the position at common law – the court found that s 1 primarily concerned 'factual investigation' about the statement's impact.[33] Lord Sumption held that to satisfy s 1 claimants must build an evidential case and adduce evidence that demonstrates that the statement(s) complained of have had a reputationally damaging impact.[34] If this is not possible, claimants may plead an inferential case, which argues that the statements are *likely* to cause serious reputational harm, with reference to a number of factors, such as: the scale of publications, that people who knew the claimant had read the statement(s), that they could come to the attention of others in future and the gravity of the statements themselves.[35] This was a controversial interpretation, as it overturned the long-standing presumption-of-damage principle for libel at common law.[36] This decision is also significant for the purposes of this book as it made clear that the bar had been firmly raised from the common law position; s 1 is now a significant hurdle for claimants to overcome and is most likely to be satisfied with hard evidence about a statement's defamatory impact, such as testimony from individuals who have read a statement and, as a result, thought less of a claimant.[37] This is not always easy to demonstrate, particularly in relation to posts on social media sites like X in the *defamation by social media* scenario, which can be more transient in nature. People reading posts behind their X 'handles' may also be reticent to come forward. This will be discussed in more detail later. Lord Sumption also found that taking into account damage to the claimant's reputation from people reading the statement who *didn't know her at the*

---

[32] Ibid [14]; emphasis added.
[33] Ibid [12] and Sewell (n 4) 54.
[34] *Lachaux v Independent Print* (n 30) [21].
[35] Ibid.
[36] Sewell (n 4) 55.
[37] *Lachaux v Independent Print* (n 30) [21].

time is also perfectly legitimate in establishing whether s 1 is met.[38] However, once again this is a difficult line of enquiry for a claimant to substantiate, as individuals who did not know them at the time of reading will scarcely know them better *after* reading the statement complained of, and once again may be both difficult to get in touch with on the part of the claimant and even more difficult to convince to come forward in the case of online posts. For the purposes of what a claimant must now prove for an actionable case in defamation, what matters most is how the *Lachaux* 'factors' have been distilled by the case law that has followed. The court in *Coker* summarizes factors that may go towards an *inferential* case: 'serious harm can in principle be proved on a combination of (a) the meaning of the words; (b) the situation of the claimant; (c) the circumstances of publication; and (d) the inherent probabilities.'[39]

However unfortunate for claimants, Lord Sumption was undoubtedly right that parliamentary intention was to 'raise the bar' in s 1, as otherwise enacting it would have been redundant. Indeed, the decision has drawn praise at least for its sound legal interpretation of the 2013 statute.[40] Despite the fact that the decision 'is legally convincing',[41] the new and far stricter interpretation of s 1 has concerning timing given the potentially unlimited defamatory potential posed by the internet, with its ease and multitude of platforms on which defamatory remarks can be spread (including social media, in the *defamation by social media* scenario – but also beyond it). Artificial intelligence (AI) programs and new mediums such as digital worlds, many of which are free to use, present new threats to reputation rights online. As a result, there is a greater

---

[38] Ibid [25].
[39] *Coker v Nwakanma* [2021] EWHC 1011 (QB) [12].
[40] David Erdos, 'Case comment: Serious harm to reputation rights? Defamation in the Supreme Court' (2019) 78(3) *Cambridge Law Journal* 510, 512.
[41] Ibid.

menace to reputation and therefore individual dignity today than ever before and this seems incongruent with parliament's recent intention to make it *more difficult* to bring an early stage claim in defamation by installing this 'control mechanism'.[42] As Erdos puts it: 'it remains the case that untrue and unfair attacks on reputation are increasing (principally online) and defamation law may often not provide an effective avenue for vindicating the rights that are thereby impaired.'[43]

This new threshold has also made case outcomes difficult to predict for claimants. Legal practitioners and academics alike are awaiting more detailed guidance (that will emerge over time) of clear themes that will demonstrate s 1 is likely met.[44] This current uncertainty creates a climate of fear for those considering litigating over a potentially reputationally harmful statement online, which is already a costly process, particularly if a claim is disposed of at an early stage due to this threshold.

c. How does one evidence serious harm caused or likely to be caused by an online post?

As explained earlier, the Supreme Court decision in *Lachaux* has set a high bar. The investigation that is now required by the courts to meet s 1 risks that 'defamation actions will become stuck in lengthy and expensive interlocutory proceedings',[45] as Erdos has observed. Overtly, an assessment of whether s 1 is met by a post, for example, on Facebook, should not be inherently different to argument that it is met by virtue of a publication in print. However, in practice, the way evidence can be adduced to meet this threshold and the type of evidence that can be offered will likely be different for a

---

[42] Sewell (n 4) 69.
[43] Erdos (n 40) 513.
[44] Sewell (n 4) 70.
[45] Erdos (n 40) 512.

post online than in print – with evidential hurdles a yet higher mountain to claim for those defamed online. A detailed recent case on s 1, *Amersi v Leslie*, noted that in order to meet s 1 the court examines a combination of the *impact the words have had* and the *inherent tendency* of the words,[46] with reference to this sentiment expressed by the Supreme Court in *Lachaux*. The High Court in *Amersi* also made a number of other salient observations. Firstly, even publication (online or otherwise) to a 'relatively small number of publishees may yet cause very serious harm to reputation'[47] – so the question is not merely one of the number of 'hits' online, although this is clearly relevant. On a sympathetic note to claimants, the court observed that in 'mass publication' cases – such as mass dissemination using a social media platform such as X – 'a claimant may struggle to identify, or produce evidence from all those to whom an article was published'.[48] Indeed, this would be an impossible task for some defamed online, where posts on X may have reached hundreds of thousands of followers. The court observed that this is perfectly acceptable – however, in cases where the matter was published to a single person, evidence would be sought and needed.[49] This may prove difficult for claimants in situations where third-party readers have been contacted privately through the 'messenger' function on Facebook with defamatory statements, perhaps by someone they do not know, so they do not necessarily want to come forward and support a claimant who has been defamed. Lord Justice Warby has also observed that in relation to online publication to strangers,

---

[46] *Amersi v Leslie* [2023] EWHC 1368 (KB) [144] and *Lachaux v Independent Print* (n 30) [14].

[47] *Amersi v Leslie* (n 46) [145]; *Sobrinho v Impresa Publishing SA* [2016] EMLR 12 [47]; *Dhir v Sadler* [2018] 4 WLR 1 [55 (i)]; *Monir v Wood* [2018] EWHC 3525 (QB) [196].

[48] *Amersi v Leslie* (n 46) [146].

[49] Ibid.

a mass of publications could engender the s 1 threshold has met – each individual publication does not have to, in itself, create serious harm to one's reputation.[50] This is clearly a logical and practical approach. However, *Amersi* noted that one cannot 'aggregate' reputational harm for the purposes of the serious harm threshold by mere generalities: 'ultimately a claimant must satisfy s.1 by evidence'[51] in respect of *each individual statement* complained of. Therefore, one cannot argue that a number of posts all relating to the claimant *as a whole* may cause serious harm to their reputation – rather, each statement complained of must be individually examined as to whether it meets this high threshold, as the High Court recently observed in *Goldsmith*.[52] This is certainly a daunting task and, in multiple-post cases concerning online speech, will lead to many posts falling at this hurdle at an early stage. This runs contrary to the fact that it would in fact make contextual sense in some *defamation by social media* cases to run posts together and for s 1 to be examined holistically – as often posts made about the same matter over a short time period are read in succession by online observers. In fact, due to the short character limit of X,[53] a defamatory meaning in fact could be observed by reading several different posts together, rather than separately – as people often label posts in the style of 'post 1 of X number'. This is also the case for short video-sharing platforms such as TikTok, where a user plays a short video clip and this is then followed by another related video that then plays immediately after – or a person can return to an uploader's homepage and click to view the next video adjacent in the viewing

---

[50] *Banks v Cadwalladr* [2023] EWCA Civ 219 [49].
[51] *Amersi v Leslie* (n 46) [162].
[52] *Goldsmith v Bissett-Powell* [2022] EWHC 1591 (QB) [152].
[53] Which for standard users is 280 characters. See https://x.com/premium/status/1623411400545632256 accessed 29 November 2024.

panel, several of which may piece together a longer, potentially defamatory, narrative.[54]

What has emerged from the case law to date is that the serious harm threshold is an exercise in fact finding, with a claimant expected to provide evidence that requisite reputational damage was caused by the complained-of statements. However, if hard evidence cannot be produced to point towards concrete damage to individual reputation (due perhaps in part to the difficulties as outlined), an inferential case can instead be pled, which argues that by *inference* it is clear that serious harm to reputation – and therefore personal dignity – has been done, or is likely to be done in the future. It is submitted that this is more likely the route to be taken in respect to claimants who are defamed online, as it may be harder to adduce hard evidence in the form of – for example – third-party reader testimony that can corroborate the claim. Unfortunately, arguing a purely inferential case is fraught with challenges and it is often more difficult to prove that the serious harm threshold has been met. In inferential cases, the *Lachaux* factors of 'the meaning of the words, the situation of claimant, the circumstances of publication and the inherent probabilities' are relevant.[55] The courts have powerfully stated that there is a difference between an inferential case and 'speculation',[56] although it is not abundantly clear what this difference is and any decision based entirely on inference is likely to involve some level of speculative thought. Particularly with cases, be they online or offline, that involve a small number of publishees, s 1 has made it extremely difficult to plead a successful inferential

---

[54] A recording can be up to ten minutes in length if one records using the TikTok function. See Camera Tools, TikTok Support, https://support.tiktok.com/en/using-tiktok/creating-videos/camera-tools accessed 29 November 2024.

[55] *Blake v Fox* [2024] EWHC 146 (KB) [50] and *Lachaux v Independent Print* (n 30) [21].

[56] *Sivananthan v Vasikaran* [2023] EMLR 7 [53].

case without hard evidence of seriously harmful defamatory impact – as the 'percolation' effects of mass publication cannot be relied on.[57] Finally, it should be noted that the single most important factor that is repeatedly relied on in defamation proceedings going to the weight of the serious harm threshold is the *seriousness of the statement complained of*.[58] This is the case regardless if defamatory allegations are spread using the internet or by other mediums. On a number of occasions, the courts have gone so far as to abandon substantive analysis of the s 1 threshold if the statement complained of is sufficiently reputationally grave – the idea being that this threshold has been implicitly met.[59] On this topic, Mr Justice Warby has stated, 'it is certainly not necessary in every case to engage in a detailed forensic examination of the precise factual picture, in order to determine whether the serious harm requirement is satisfied'.[60] An obvious question remains: exactly how serious do allegations have to be to negate the fact-finding exercise of s 1's threshold? The answer, unhelpfully, is as yet unclear – offering little comfort to claimants and defendants alike. Perhaps unsurprisingly, early studies have found that imputations of morally reprehensible conduct, such as sexual impropriety or conduct striking to the core of one's personality, are more likely to result in s 1 as met.[61]

d. What is the significance of viewership and engagement metrics to s 1?

In light of the reform in s 1, the courts have struggled with the question of the precise significance of online viewership or engagement metrics of a defamatory post. Several decisions

---

[57] *Amersi v Leslie* (n 46) [159].
[58] Sewell (n 4) 58–60.
[59] See, for example, *Coker v Nwakanma* (n 39) [33].
[60] *Monroe v Hopkins* (n 22) [69].
[61] Sewell (n 4) 58–60.

have been at pains to stress that satisfying the threshold 'was never just a "numbers game": one well directed arrow [may] hit the bull's eye of reputation'.[62] Despite this, in reality, many cases that concern *defamation by social media* consider engagement metrics as relevant to the threshold being met. In the recent case of *Bukhari v Bukhari*, which related to a number of posts on X that alleged the claimants were criminals, counsel for the claimant argued that the defendant had nearly 2,000 followers and 'tagged' other individuals in the posts, including one that had millions of followers – in an attempt to satisfy s 1.[63] Counsel also argued that the view count of each post was relevant, including the number of 'likes' and re-posts.[64] Further, in *Hayden v Family Education Trust*, which again concerned a comment on X, the numbers of re-posts, account followers, those who were 'tagged' and how long the post remained on X all were found to be crucial to the assessment of whether the serious harm threshold was met.[65] A total of 3,800 followers on X was deemed to be significant for the purposes of s 1, as was the total extent of the publication on X to 45,000 users.[66] It was also deemed relevant that there was a 'social media and mainstream media frenzy' which coincided, driving people to X – demonstrating that claims in respect to online posts can also be bolstered by traditional media coverage. Importantly, *Hayden* noted a number of things in relation to social media posts and the s 1 threshold. Firstly, the duration of the post is important to determining analytics – if a post is only available for a short time and then deleted, even if there is a large follower base, it will be harder to obtain representative analytics but also to prove a large breadth of publication, as not every

---

[62] *Amersi v Leslie* (n 46) [145] quoting *King v Grundon* [2012] EWHC 2719 (QB) [40].
[63] [2023] EWHC 427 (KB) [87].
[64] Ibid.
[65] *Hayden v Family Education Trust* [2023] EWHC 950 (KB) [2] and [8].
[66] Ibid [8].

follower will seen the post in the narrow time period it was available.[67] This poses an additional problem for claimants, as it allows defendants to (perhaps strategically) post a potentially reputationally damaging statement on social media for a short time but then quickly delete it, the swift deletion leading to the serious harm threshold being difficult to prove on the part of a claimant on whom the burden firmly lies.[68] This approach does little to deter defamation online in the digital age. Numbers of social media 'followers' was also seen as strongly relevant to the determination of the s 1 threshold in *Miller v Turner*, where 16 posts on X and a webpage were complained of.[69] There is, then, a clear disconnect here – some members of the judiciary have claimed that decisions about the serious harm threshold are not a 'numbers game', yet social media analytics seem to be playing a pivotal role in how the serious harm threshold is decided in online defamation cases. Using analytics in this way is a somewhat reductive exercise and it is hard to believe that this is what parliament exactly envisaged when enacting s 1. The court in *Wright v Granath* found that expert evidence about how many people read a tweet is not expected or necessary,[70] although it is noted here that given a judicial lack of technological expertise in certain cases it might be – notwithstanding the time and economic cost that comes with it.

However, not all decisions regarding the serious harm threshold and posts on social media have rendered problematic results for claimants – certain judges have led the way with practical and technologically insightful decisions. Several cases have correctly observed that *readership* numbers are often larger than engagement numbers of an online post, as no account

---

[67] Ibid [34].
[68] Ibid [43].
[69] *Miller, Power v Turner* [2023] EWHC 2799 (KB) [47].
[70] *Wright v Granath* [2022] EWHC 1181 (QB) [59].

is required to read posts on Twitter/X.[71] The court in *Riley* observed that tweets can also be subject to a 'percolation' effect (otherwise known as the 'grapevine' effect) that inflates estimated readership numbers beyond those which pure analytics derived from social media websites suggest.[72] This takes into account the popularity or craze that surrounds certain online disputes and posts – which generates more readership traffic to these types of statements online than can be reflected in 'pure' analytics. Certain decisions have also taken into account whether a defendant's social media account was growing at the time of publication (and therefore readership wider than usual).[73] In a logical approach, the court in *Packham* found that replies to tweets can help to evidence serious harm as met,[74] as replies represent the tweets' impact on the readership without necessitating individual testimony in court. A more pragmatic approach than pure analytics alone was also suggested in the recent case of *Blake v Fox*.[75] After considering the inferential case to s 1, the court then looked at the actual *state of affairs on the ground at the time*: what people on X were saying and likely thought of Laurence Fox, if people actually believed that his statement was a rhetorical device and what newspapers were writing, in order to establish if serious harm had been caused to the claimant's reputation.[76] Influence of the particular defendant's opinions (on social media) in a particular nexus of society has also been held to be relevant to establishing s 1.[77] These are all logical factors for consideration rooted in the practicalities of proving the serious harm threshold as met for the purposes of online defamation. It is hoped that more

---

[71] If the profile is not restricted, or 'private'. Ibid [38(b)].
[72] *Riley v Murray* [2022] EMLR 8.
[73] *Wright v Granath* (n 70) [54].
[74] *Packham v Wightman* [2023] EWHC 1256 (KB) [74].
[75] *Blake v Fox* (n 55) [50].
[76] Ibid [79]–[103].
[77] *Miller, Power v Turner* (n 69) [47].

decisions in this spirit will be handed down by the courts in future and an approach wholly centred around analytics be abandoned.

e. Is there a different approach to s 1 where the internet is concerned?

Aside from different ways that claimants in online defamation cases must currently *plead* s 1 (for example, by adducing corroborating social media metrics in the *defamation by social media* scenario), there is also some evidence to suggest that the judiciary *treat* defamation on the internet differently to defamation through traditional mediums. Most famously, the Supreme Court in *Stocker v Stocker* found that Facebook: '[is] a casual medium; it is in the nature of conversation rather than carefully chosen expression; and that it is pre-eminently one in which the reader reads and passes on.'[78]

This author has argued elsewhere that this was an unfortunate choice of words on the part of Lord Kerr, as the (perhaps unintentional) implication was that social media websites are inherently transitory mediums – and therefore should be taken less seriously in terms of defamatory potential by the courts. Today, this is clearly out of step with the realities of modern media. Many people now reverently and earnestly read news through social media websites and take certain comments posted on platforms such as Facebook and X extremely seriously.[79] As the present author has argued elsewhere,[80]

---

[78] *Stocker v Stocker* [2019] UKSC 17 [43].

[79] In 2024, Ofcom reported that over half of adults use social media to find out news. Dan Milmo, 'Internet replaces TV as UK's most popular news source for first time' *The Guardian* (10 September 2024) www.theguardian.com/media/article/2024/sep/10/internet-tv-uk-most-popular-news-source-first-time#:~:text=More%20than%20half%20of%20UK,used%20by%2018%25%20of%20adults accessed 2 December 2024.

[80] Fiona Brimblecombe, '*Stocker v Stocker*' in Lewis Graham and Jennifer Russell (eds), *The Supreme Court at 15: Reflections on Private Law* (Routledge 2025).

this statement of Lord Kerr has not proved fatal to online defamation litigation. It has been easy to sidestep any inference of the Supreme Court to this effect by stating that, in the relevant circumstances, the given statement *was* in fact sufficiently serious in impacting the claimant's reputation. The Court of Appeal has also recently explicitly acknowledged in *Blake v Fox* that not all tweets are 'conversational' – with many instead presenting purported facts, designed to be taken seriously.[81] Similarly, in *Miller*, Mrs Justice Collins Rice stated when discussing Twitter/X: 'It tends to be thought of as largely consequence-free for Real Life, and so is sometimes described as a playground. But it has given a new meaning to the word 'troll' in the English language. And online behaviour *can and does have real life consequences.*'[82]

In *Banks v Cadwalladr*, the court distilled a number of overarching factors that can add to the weight of s 1 being met, reminiscent of Lord Nicholls' 'laundry list' in *Reynolds*.[83] Many of these have been discussed earlier in this chapter. For the sake of completeness, an abbreviated version of this list goes as such: s 1 is a higher threshold; each statement must meet s 1 individually; there is no presumption of serious harm; the question is of the 'actual impact' of the statement; the reactions of others are valid; evidence in proving harm is persuasive; 'sometimes inference may be enough'; bad reputation of the claimant is relevant; background context is relevant; extent of publication is relevant and malice is *not* relevant on the part of the defendant.[84] In addition to this already lengthy list, a number of other factors can also be distilled from the early case of *Monroe* that relate specifically to posts on social media and s 1. These are:

---

[81] *Blake v Fox* n 6 [67].

[82] *Miller, Power v Turner* (n 69) [5]; emphasis added.

[83] *Reynolds v Times Newspapers* [2001] 2 AC 127 [205].

[84] *Banks v Cadwalladr* [2022] EWHC 1417 (QB) [51].

1. If the post is transient, and how often it has been viewed.
2. The 'credibility' of a publisher 'in the eyes of publishees'.
3. Any evidence that 'no harm was done' to the claimant's reputation, based on 'contemporaneous social media activity'.
4. If the claimant suffered a 'torrent of abuse' as a result of the post/s.
5. The claimant's own responses on social media.
6. Any other (non-social media) coverage of the post complained of.[85]

The problem with this list is that it is a rather leading one that is skewed against finding that the s 1 threshold is met by social media posts. The point about transience is problematic as it invokes the need to employ user metrics, which are not only unreliable but also sometimes difficult to find, as discussed earlier. Credibility may also be an additional barrier for online posts to meet, as one would then be forced to argue that the person making the post had considerable social pull or sway – which may not always be possible for claimants, with the post nevertheless reputationally damaging. Similarly, it is hard to understand how a court could accurately adduce if 'no harm was done' to a claimant by other contemporaneous social media activity – as for every supportive message a claimant might receive, many other individuals who now think poorly of the claimant may have stayed silent. Factor 4 seems to suggest that a 'torrent of abuse' is another necessary hurdle that a claimant must overcome, which will not always be provable at that particular moment in time – and is also an unreasonably high bar. Finally, factor 5 seems to suggest that a claimant can in fact themselves 'put the facts straight' on social media by combatting the defamatory content posted by another – which is arguably not a claimant's responsibility, nor something they may be in the position to do. Indeed, this flies against the very purpose of

---

[85] *Monroe v Hopkins* (n 22) [71, (2)–(10)].

defamation law itself – that it justifies a restriction to freedom of expression in the face of maintaining individual reputation and, with it, personal dignity. It is hard to see how personal dignity is upheld by the idea that a claimant is expected to wrestle in a virtual mud fight with a defendant online, in a futile attempt to uphold their own (damaged) reputation as a result of a defamatory post.

f. Section 1's introduction in the context of the codified defences in the 2013 Act

It is beyond the scope of this work to consider all of the many changes ushered in by the Defamation Act 2013, most with the aim of bolstering freedom of expression. However, it is important to acknowledge another relevant change that was brought in alongside the introduction of the serious harm threshold: the codification into statute of three long-standing common law defences to defamation. The truth defence is now contained in s 2 Defamation Act 2013, although largely unchanged.[86] What was previously known as the *Reynolds* defence of responsible journalism at common law is now s 4 of the Defamation Act 2013, 'publication on matter of public interest'. The defence of fair comment became 'honest opinion', set out in s 3 of the 2013 Act. In its codification, s 3 dropped the requirement existent at common law that the opinion at issue had to be on a matter of public interest and,[87] unlike fair comment, the new defence is not defeated by malice.[88] The abolition of the public interest requirement provides a not insignificant extension to the types of statements that can be covered by the defence, which was already 'wide' at common

---

[86] Also see s 5 Defamation Act 1952 (repealed by the 2013 Act).
[87] This does not appear in the (lengthy) text of s 3 as a requirement. On the 'old' position, see: *Joseph v Spiller* [2010] UKSC 53 [3], which refers to *Tse Wai Chun Paul v Albert Cheng* [2001] EMLR 777 [16].
[88] *Joseph v Spiller* (n 87) [4].

law. Indeed, in the recent case of *Dyson*, Mr Justice Kay observed that 'the scope for honest comment, however wounding and unbalanced, was very considerable indeed'.[89] Lowering the bar for defendants attempting to use the defence of honest opinion in tandem with raising the bar for claimants through the introduction of the serious harm threshold results in an undeniable impediment to those wishing in bring an action in defamation, with respect to online content or otherwise. It should, however, be noted that despite this change in s 3, recent cases such as *Butt*, *Dyson* and *Blake* have shown that honest opinion will in many ways be interpreted in a similar fashion to its predecessor, fair comment.[90] Pre-2013 Act case law was extensively used to reach the decision in *Dyson*, while in *Blake* the court reaffirmed the traditional distinction between fact and opinion, finding opinion to be a 'deduction'[91] in a manner consistent with the pre-2013 decision of *Singh*.[92]

The defence that poses a more significant problem for claimants post-2013 codification is s 4. Perhaps unsurprisingly, it is this defence has altered the most from its common law predecessor. At common law, the *Reynolds* defence offered protection for investigative journalists publishing pieces in the public interest that could not be shown to be true (at least to the standard of 'justification' or the truth defence). The defence therefore filled a gap in the law, allowing journalists to publish important stories that the public ought to know, free from the fear of libel. The standard set for reliance on the *Reynolds* defence was that of responsible journalism and it was applied with reference to Lord Nicholls' famous ten-factor list set out in the case of *Reynolds* itself.[93] The

---

[89] *Dyson v MGN Ltd* [2023] EWHC 3092 (KB) [144].
[90] *Dr Salman Butt v The Secretary of State for the Home Department* [2019] EWCA Civ 933, *Dyson v MGN* (n 89), and *Blake v Fox* (n 6).
[91] *Blake v Fox* (n 6) [23].
[92] *British Chiropractic Association v Singh* [2010] EWCA Civ 350.
[93] *Reynolds v Times Newspapers* (n 83) [205].

factors included: the seriousness of the allegation, its nature, source, whether verification was sought, its status, urgency, whether comment was sought from the claimant, whether the claimant's side of the story was put forth, tone, and circumstances of the publication.[94] *Reynolds* quickly embedded itself as an important defence and generated a range of case law. It is important to note that *Reynolds*, at the most basic level, was about the public's *right to know* certain information and the precise circumstances in which journalists could evade liability in defamation on that basis.[95] The precise scope of the defence was later qualified in a patchwork way by cases that came after *Reynolds*: *Jameel v Wall Street Journal* reaffirmed Lord Nicholls' earlier position that his list of factors should not be treated as an exhaustive set of hurdles, all of which must be overcome to bring a claim.[96] The factors added to the weight of proving responsible journalism had taken place.[97] However, the defence was not without its critics – and in the Libel Reform Campaign, spearheaded by journalists and human rights campaigners as well as scientists, it was argued that the defence was seen as unfairly complex and too difficult to rely on.[98] As a result of the successful lobbying of this campaign, the s 4 defence was born. *Reynolds* and its rich case law was substantively abolished and replaced instead with a two-pronged test in s 4.[99] Firstly, the court must consider whether the information was in the public interest.[100] If the

---

[94] Ibid factors 1–10 in order.
[95] Jenny Steele, *Tort Law* (1st edn, OUP 2007) 789–90. Credit should also be given to Professor Richard Mullender for elucidating this point in lectures given circa 2013 on the matter at Newcastle Law School, UK.
[96] *Jameel v Wall Street Journal (No 2)* [2006] UKHL 44 [33].
[97] Ibid [32].
[98] House of Lords and House of Commons Joint Committee on the Draft Defamation Bill Session 2010–12, Report (12 October 2011) 8, 22, 27.
[99] Section 4(6) Defamation Act 2013.
[100] Section 4(1)(a) Defamation Act 2013.

answer is affirmative, then the second relevant question is whether the publisher *reasonably believed* that publication was in the public interest.[101]

The replacement of *Reynolds*' rich body of precedent by s 4 has resulted in a number of negative ramifications for the law.[102] Firstly, this author has argued elsewhere that legal clarity for both claimants and defendants has been sacrificed at the altar to appease the Libel Reform Campaign through the enactment of s 4.[103] This is largely because s 4 is too short and it is unclear what the new standard to rely on s 4 *actually is*. Unfortunately, detailed and authoritative guidance from senior courts is still awaited. The Supreme Court in *Serafin* did little to clarify the precise content and scope of the new test in s 4, although Lord Wilson made it clear that s 4 was intended to operate differently and more flexibly to *Reynolds* at common law (but not precisely how).[104] Secondly, reference to responsible journalism in the Act was departed from in order to broaden the scope of the defence and the circumstances in which the defence could be relied upon. Regardless of the merits of this endeavour, this has resulted in complex legal questions that are yet to be answered – it is not yet apparent quite *how broadly* the judiciary will be prepared to interpret s 4. Early indications have shown that s 4 can be applied to a wide range of contextual scenarios, including those where the defendant has no formal (or even informal) journalistic training and is in fact engaging in a

---

[101] Section 4(1)(b) Defamation Act 2013.

[102] To make matters more confusing, the Explanatory Notes to the 2013 also state that *Reynolds* case law is relevant in an advisory capacity to interpreting s 4: leading some to comment that the defence has only been 'pseudo-codified'. See Fiona Brimblecombe, 'Section 4 Defamation Act 2013: A tale of two approaches' (2024) 29 *Torts Law Journal* 245, Part C, fn 148.

[103] Brimblecombe (n 102).

[104] *Serafin v Malkiewicz* [2020] UKSC 23 [57].

process very far removed from responsible journalism, from which this defence originated. Two prevalent examples where this has occurred are the cases of *Economou* and *Hay*.[105] In *Economou*, de Freitas' daughter had falsely accused Economou of rape and the Crown Prosecution Service were preparing to mount a case against her for perverting the course of justice before she took her own life.[106] On receiving legal advice, de Freitas had supplied information to the press about the matter, including defamatory allegations about Economou, resulting in a number of news articles and broadcasts.[107] Economou brought an action in defamation against de Freitas. The Court of Appeal in the matter allowed de Freitas to successfully rely on the s 4 defence and in so doing extended its scope to encompass what has been dubbed 'contributor immunity'.[108] Further, in the case of *Hay*, it was found that the defendant could rely on the s 4 defence for acting in ways that were merely vaguely reminiscent of an investigative journalist,[109] such as the fact the defendant had undertaken her own informal enquiries and the lack of cooperation of the police in the matter.[110] The case also seems to suggest that because the defendant was writing from her own experiences, that the idea of the information's verification (itself a *Reynolds* factor) should be approached

---

[105] *Economou v de Frietas* [2016] EWHC 1853 (QB) and *Economou v de Frietas* [2018] EWCA Civ 2591. *Hay v Cresswell* [2023] EWHC 882 (KB).

[106] *Economou v de Frietas* [2018] (n 105) [1]–[9].

[107] Information which de Freitas ardently believed was true. Ibid and see Dominic Garner, 'Case law: *Economou v de Freitas*, Court of Appeal guidance on "public interest" defence' (*Inforrm*, 5 December 2018) https://inforrm.org/2018/12/05/case-law-economou-v-de-freitas-court-of-appeal-guidance-on-public-interest-defence-dominic-garner/ accessed 11 September 2019.

[108] Garner (n 107) and *Economou v de Frietas* [2018] (n 105) [107].

[109] *Hay v Cresswell* (n 105).

[110] Ibid [210, vi].

in a more generous capacity,[111] favourable to a defendant. The turn of s 4 to the expansive is not surprising, as the whole point of jettisoning *Reynolds* at common law and its replacement with s 4 was to extend the scope of the defence and give it a more flexible nature[112] – although the outer limits of the defence as yet remain unclear and unexplained by the judiciary.

It is beyond the scope of this chapter to discuss this matter further and these are just two cases that evidence the potential breadth of the s 4 defence since reform. It is fair to say that the expanding nature of the (now statutory) defences alongside the introduction of the s 1 serious harm threshold has created a problem for claimants in defamation. To add yet more confusion, it appears that s 1 and s 4 at times may yield an interaction: if protection afforded by the s 4 defence in a later 'phase' of publication is found to fall away, it has been held that s 1 may also need reassessment at a later stage of publication. In *Banks v Cadwalladr*, it was found that reliance on s 4 as a defence ought to be reassessed at different points in 'phases' of publication – the defence falling away after new facts came to light which removed a finding of reasonable belief under s 4(1)(b).[113] It was also found in *Banks* that s 1 would also need to be reassessed in light of this, as the contextual circumstances of the later phase of publication had changed.[114] In other words, even if a claimant has successfully argued that s 1 has been met at the outset of a claim (a particularly difficult task for victims of online defamation), if circumstances change in a publication's timeline, then the s 1 threshold may still need to be reassessed.

---

[111] Ibid [210, xviii].
[112] Lord McNally HL, Grand Committee, vol 741 col 534, and *Serafin* (n 104) [65].
[113] *Banks v Cadwalladr* (n 50).
[114] Ibid [47] and [48].

II. Concluding remarks about s 1 and online defamation

To conclude this section, it is fitting to restate a number of findings from the analysis given about why it may be harder to meet the s 1 threshold in the *defamation by social media* scenario.

1. *Section 1(1) 'raising the bar' has meant that the most effective way to argue that the threshold is met is by the 'evidentiary' route*, providing supporting evidence that shows that the claimant's reputation has been harmed by the post in question. One way to do this is to physically bring people to trial to testify that they thought less of the claimant as a result of the post in question. While this may be hard to do for any claimant, it is particularly challenging in respect of information posted to social media or other websites – as readers may be anonymous, difficult to get hold of, live geographically far away or be less likely to respond to a request to take part in the trial.[115]
2. *It is difficult to know the exact reach of a defamatory post on a publicly available website or social media*, a factor that adds to the weight of s 1 being met – and discussed in three-quarters of judgments.[116] When magazines are sold, this gives a clear idea of how many copies are in the public domain; this is not the case with website 'hits'. Many hits might be from the same small group of people. It may also prove challenging to ascertain where those hits geographically came from, unless IP addresses are tracked – and in any event, people could be using a virtual private network to disguise their location.
3. *Judges have held that proving s 1(1) as satisfied is not merely a 'numbers game', but when online posts are scrutinized for the purposes of the threshold, this often leads to user metrics being*

---

[115] Sewell (n 4) 60.
[116] Ibid.

adduced – and the precise size of the numbers involved is a significant contributing factor to finding s 1 is met.[117] A reliance on user metrics to this extent is a reductive exercise. Such metrics can also be unreliable as numbers of views do not always correlate to accurately to post readership, especially when posts are viewable in the public domain and not through a logged-in network. Despite this, the courts seem preoccupied with the usage of metrics in online defamation cases to the detriment of other relevant factors. Posts can also be deleted, and with this, valuable information about readership may be lost – which can lead to s 1 failing to be met, a burden which is on the claimant to prove.[118]

4. *Certain cases have found that the s 1 threshold has to be met by each individual statement complained of* rather than holistically if several posts are involved. This fails to take into account that if several successive posts are published around the same time frame, it is likely many of the same readers will have been exposed to all of them – and therefore may form a rounded defamatory impression of the claimant as a result of the *combination* of the posts. The court has also found that s 1 threshold also has to *be re-examined at different publication phases*.[119] This can lead to a finding of s 1 as met falling away at a later stage of proceedings. It should be noted that this is more likely to happen with regards to discussions taking place on social media, where new information comes to light typically more quickly as it can be shared instantly.

5. *There is some indication certain members of the judiciary may harbour a level of inherent scepticism about defamation online*, and information conveyed on social media may be viewed as less serious than information conveyed in a newspaper

---

[117] *Amersi v Leslie* (n 46) [145] quoting *King v Grundon* (n 62) [40].
[118] Sewell (n 4) 64.
[119] *Banks v Cadwalladr* (n 50) [5].

or other forms of traditional media.[120] When this scepticism is apparent, it can mean that claimant counsel has to work harder to convince a judge that s 1 has been met in the case – but have less avenues to do so as the information has been disseminated through the internet, where it is more challenging to get hard evidence about its impact and reach.

III. The introduction of the single publication rule in s 8 Defamation Act 2013

a. Background to s 8

The single publication rule introduced by the 2013 Act was a truly new addition to libel's legal framework, unlike the serious harm threshold, which was, rather, a stricter interpretation of common law rules that came before it. Section 8 replaces the previous common law position, the multiple publication rule, which termed that each new republication of a defamatory statement by a publisher can yield a fresh claim. By pro-reform campaigners, the multiple publication rule was considered to be unduly skewed towards reputational interests, potentially creating crushing liability on defendants.[121] This is despite the fact that the rule had a clear reason behind its operation; that each subsequent republication, no matter how much later in time, can yield fresh reputational harm – particularly if it is brought to new audiences. The rule itself originated from the famed case of *Brunswick v Harmer*, which concerned a 17-year-old newspaper with libellous content being sold, giving rise to a new claim – with its own limitation period

---

[120] *Stocker v Stocker* (n 78) [43].

[121] Alastair Mullis and Andrew Scott, 'Tilting at windmills: The Defamation Act 2013' (2014) 77(1) *Modern Law Review* 87, 102.

of one year as generated.[122] The previous position of the law helped to shield individual dignity, the very interest that lies at the heart of reputation's protection in the law. Much like the introduction of the serious harm threshold, this change is yet another example of the 2013 reform's pivot towards Article 10 ECHR interests. The single publication rule in s 8 instead introduces a limitation period of one year, time running from the *first* publication of a defamatory statement by a publisher. If the publisher then later republishes the statement in 'substantially the same'[123] form and an action cannot be brought within this one-year window (from the first publication) then an action is effectively prohibited. Mr Justice Warby states the new rule simply: 'a claim in respect of a defamatory statement is barred once a year has passed since its first publication by the defendant'.[124]

This, of course, may cause problems for individuals looking to action *repetition of statements online over a year later* in the scenario outlined in Chapter 2. Another reason given for single publication rule's introduction was that the law as it stood would freeze the operation of web archives, with the operators of such archives repeatedly exposed to 'fresh' claims in defamation every time information was accessed – however old.[125] The Privy Council explains it as such:

> The effect of section 8 of the 2013 Act in English law is therefore that a claimant has one year from the first

---

[122] *Duke of Brunswick v Harmer* (n 1); *Loutchansky v Times Newspapers Ltd (No 2)* [2001] EWCA Civ 1805, [2002] QB 783 [57] and Defamation Act 2013. Explanatory Notes, UK Public General Acts, 2013 c 26, Commentary on Sections, Section 8: Single publication rule [60] www.legislation.gov.uk/ukpga/2013/26/notes/division/5/8 accessed 1 December 2024.

[123] Section 8(1)(b) Defamation Act 2013.

[124] *Richardson v Facebook, Google* [2015] EWHC 3154 (QB) [49].

[125] Mullis and Scott (n 121) 102.

publication of the libel to bring proceedings, however many times the libel is later repeated. This changed the common law position, according to which each publication of a libel gave rise to a separate cause of action with its own one year limitation period ...[126]

Section 8 is only short, stating:

(1) This section applies if a person –
   (a) publishes a statement to the public ("the first publication"), and
   (b) subsequently publishes (whether or not to the public) that statement or a statement which is substantially the same.
(2) In subsection (1) "publication to the public" includes publication to a section of the public.
(3) For the purposes of section 4A of the Limitation Act 1980 (time limit for actions for defamation etc) any cause of action against the person for defamation in respect of the subsequent publication is to be treated as having accrued on the date of the first publication.
(4) This section does not apply in relation to the subsequent publication if the manner of that publication is *materially different* from the manner of the first publication.
(5) In determining whether the manner of a subsequent publication is materially different from the manner of the first publication, the matters to which the court may have regard include (amongst other matters) –
   (a) the level of prominence that a statement is given;
   (b) the extent of the subsequent publication.[127]

---

[126] *Hilaire v Chastanet (PC)* [2023] UKPC 22 [53].
[127] Section 8 Defamation Act 2013; emphasis added.

The rule is not based on legal principle, but rather policy. It is a '"legal fiction" crafted to simplify litigation'[128] and reduce it – thereby prioritizing the rights of defendants and freedom of expression. This is despite the fact that online defamation is on the rise and the chance of a statement being repeated online – whether or not it was initially disseminated through the internet by the same publisher – may be high (invoking the *repetition of statements online over a year later* scenario). Interestingly, the new rule mimics a similar rule in American defamation law. This is, of course, a legal system famously swayed in favour of the sacrosanct importance of freedom of speech due to the First Amendment, which does not view reputation as an equal yet competing right. This is unlike the ECHR, which puts both reputation (protected by Article 8) and expression (Article 10) on an equal footing as qualified rights, which is of course the relevant framework for English law. The single publication rule in the US is derived from the common law, but also the Second Restatement of Torts in 1977 and the Uniform Single Publication Act 1952.[129] Much like s 8, the single publication rule in the US works by the limitation period beginning to run 'when a statement is first published'.[130] Harder notes that the US Court of Appeal in New Orleans found in 2007 that the single publication rule also applies to statements published online.[131] Earlier, in 2002, the landmark ruling of *Firth v State* demonstrated a willingness of the American courts to show that the historical, entrenched rules of US defamation law would be applied to online publications as well,[132] similarly holding

---

[128] Lori A. Wood, 'Cyber-defamation and the single publication rule' (2001) 81(4) *Boston University Law Review* 895, 898.

[129] Ibid 897.

[130] Amy Harder, 'When defamation goes online: Courts are increasingly applying the single publication rule to online publications to deter stale lawsuits' (2008) *The News Media & The Law* 37.

[131] Ibid.

[132] 98 N.Y.2d 365, 775 N.E.2d 463, 747 N.Y.S.2d 69 (2002).

that the single publication rule – with its limitation period of one year – would apply to online posts.[133] In statutory form, the Defamation Act 2013 adopts the more draconian American approach of barring claims after a year has run, regardless of any further reputationally damaging impact on a claimant through successive republication by a publisher and seemingly regardless of the competing interests of a claimant and the defamatory potential of the internet.

b. Thin justifications

As referred to earlier, one of the reasons given for s 8's adoption was to protect those who operated web archives; there was a concern that the pre-existing common law position would curtail archive potential and speech online as a result.[134] Others have likewise argued that without the single publication rule search engines like Google may also be regularly actioned against, which has the potential to dredge up defamatory content from many years ago.[135] This is the famed 'floodgates' argument in tort law, that indeterminate liability of an uncontrolled nature should be restricted at common law on the grounds of policy, rooted in fairness for defendants, avoidance of crushing liability and practicalities. This is also the argument behind the continued use of the rule in the US,[136] Harder observing that 'the purpose of the single-publication rule is to safeguard publishers against endless liability'.[137]

However, it is important to consider if enacting s 8 was the only option to avoid this eventuality or if another way could

---

[133] Alan J. Pierce, 'New York's appellate courts wrestle with significant issues in internet defamation cases' (2013) 17(4) *Journal of Internet Law* 1, 9.

[134] Mullis and Scott (n 121) 102.

[135] Notwithstanding any operation of the s 5 Defence of Operators of Websites in the Defamation Act 2013 (discussed in Chapter 4).

[136] Pierce (n 133) 12.

[137] Harder (n 130) 37.

have been used. If the reason the single publication rule in the English jurisdiction was (at least in part) based on the desire to maintain the operation of online archives, there were other options that could have been used to safeguard online archivists. Firstly, such operators may have been protected already, if content on the archiving websites had been posted by third parties.[138] If this was not the case – and the content was instead uploaded (even if not authored) by the archivists themselves, then a new defence similar to that in s 5 Defamation Act 2013 could have been drafted to protect online archivists who did not reasonably believe that the documents being archived contained defamatory material; and in the event they were made aware of this, acted appropriately swiftly to remove the information using a notification-and-takedown mechanism. A parallel could easily have been drawn with the rule in *Vizetelly v Mudie's Select Library*,[139] where it was held that even large libraries are expected to take reasonable care regarding republishing defamatory statements of another in books provided in order to be protected from a defamation suit. If this approach was unfavourable, a blanket defence (suitably specific and narrow) regarding online archivists in the pursuance of academic interest and with no malicious intent could have also been drafted. Yet instead, due to the pressure of the reform campaign, parliament chose to impose s 8, which prohibits *all* claims seeking action on republication of a defamatory statement by the same publisher over a year later, thereby impacting reputational interests in a much broader, general fashion. When interviewed by Harder, a US lawyer commented on the court's decision to apply the single publication rule to online posts, stating 'there really wasn't any reason to go a different way'.[140] This ignores the very real threat to individual reputation posed by

---

[138] By virtue of s 5 Defamation Act 2013.
[139] *Vizetelly v Mudie's Select Library* [1900] 2 QB 170.
[140] Harder (n 130) 37.

the dissemination capabilities of the internet and the ease and scale by which information can be republished to the masses online, damaging individual reputations repeatedly. Further, when one examines justifications for operating the rule in a US context, it is plain to see that many such justifications do not apply to the English jurisdiction. Wood has observed that the American rule is concerned with

> preventing a plaintiff from bringing numerous suits concerning the same publication. Instead, the rule folds the claims from all applicable jurisdictions into one claim. In addition, the rule precludes the recovery of excessive damages, a possible result of numerous suits resources by preventing depletion through duplicative actions.[141]

The multiple jurisdiction issue applies to the US as different suits can be opened in different states, an issue which is not applicable to the English and Welsh jurisdiction. Wood's second observation – that the rule in part bars crushing liability through the recovery of excessive damages – also fails to translate to the English legal system, where monetary damages are typically far lower than in the US. As these justifications fall away, and the online archive issue could have been dealt with by other legal means, it is hard to understand why it was necessary to enact such a draconian shift to the law with s 8 when online libel is more prevalent than ever before. The central problem with the single publication rule in s 8 is that it tips too far in favour of expression, with the potential to bar redress and the protection of Article 8 interests. Phillipson has called for an 'equitable' reinterpretation of s 8 by the courts, using s 3 of the Human Rights Act 1998 to give

---

[141] Wood (n 128) 898.

credence to Article 8 concerns.[142] At the time of writing, this unfortunately has not come to fruition, and seems unlikely to do so.

c. What is republication in 'substantially the same' form?

If one examines the text of s 8, there is a clear caveat to its operation. It only applies to defamatory statements as (re)published if they are 'substantially the same'.[143] It goes on to stress that the section is not applicable if the second publication is 'materially different' from the first publication.[144] It has not been clarified to date by the courts what publishing something in substantially the same form actually looks like, nor how different a publication must be to be considered materially different. Under the US single publication rule, it would require 'a substantial modification of the same version',[145] as 'merely adding nonsubstantive material' would not suffice.[146] This is an extremely high bar for claimants to meet, but there is no evidence as yet that this will be the English position adopted under s 8 – and it is submitted here it should not be. A sympathetic reading of the extent of difference required under s 8 to disapply the limitation period may be necessary in order that a claimant can seek redress under the *repetition of statements online over a year later* scenario. This would at the very least go some way

---

[142] Gavin Phillipson, 'The "global pariah", the Defamation Bill and the Human Rights Act' (2012) 63(1) *Northern Ireland Legal Quarterly* 149, 182.
[143] Section 8(1)(b) Defamation Act 2013.
[144] Section 8(4) Defamation Act 2013.
[145] Notes, 'The single publication rule and online copyright: Tensions between broadcast, licensing, and defamation law' (2010) 123(5) *Harvard Law Review* 1315, 1317, and see *Atkinson v McLaughlin*, 462 F Supp 2 d 1038, 1052 (DND 2006); *Nichols v Moore*, 334 F Supp 2d 944, 952 (ED Mich 2004).
[146] Notes (n 145) 1318.

to readdress the balance between the rights of defendants and ability of claimants to bring a suit in light of the limitless defamatory potential of the internet.

Phillipson has argued that republishing something on the internet when it has previously been published in traditional media should constitute a material difference for the purposes of negating s 8, as placing something on the internet has the potential to do new and significant reputational damage, although this was not a view shared by the Joint Committee on the (then) Defamation Bill.[147] Kumar agrees with Phillipson's proposition, on the basis that the statement, when republished online, will reach a 'new audience'.[148] Aside from this, the manner of publication moving from (for example) paper print to the internet is clearly also physically different from a pragmatic perspective. Perhaps surprisingly, this view is consistent with the US approach to the single publication rule, as this qualifies as a 'republication exemption',[149] as putting something online 'reaches a new group'[150] and is therefore classed as a new and separate publication, as it is 'the result of a conscious independent act'.[151] While this is logically and principally is the legally correct approach, any contrary finding with regards to s 8 (as suggested by the Defamation Bill's Joint Committee)[152] would in fact find English defamation law is going *further* to shield defendants and disadvantage claimants than US law, despite the operation of the ECHR in the English jurisdiction.

---

[147] Phillipson (n 142) 182.

[148] Sapna Kumar, 'Comment: Website libel and the single publication rule' (2003) 70 *University of Chicago Law Review* 639, 657–9 and Notes (n 145) 1319.

[149] Wood (n 128) 901.

[150] Ibid.

[151] Notes (n 145) 1318 and *Lehman v Discovery Commc'ns, Inc*, 332 F Supp 2d 534, 539 (EDNY 2004).

[152] Phillipson (n 142) 182.

Much like the s 1 threshold, the introduction of s 8's limitation period could not have come at a worse time for those seeking to litigate about reputational damage caused by an online publication. Defamation can now happen instantaneously, easily and frequently on the internet – yet a claimant may be barred from bringing an action against a republication of an online post if the court views the statement as substantially the same. In order to mitigate disadvantages to claimants in this scenario, it is argued here that courts must interpret 'substantially the same' under Article 8(1)(b) to include exact copies of the statement, but not posts that have been otherwise changed in terms of content and format. This could include something published in a shorter, abridged version or presented in a different way – s 8(5)(a) suggests itself that a change to presentation could warrant a finding that s 8 is disapplied.[153] It is argued here that the bar for what constitutes a change in presentation should be not set too highly. This liberal interpretation would be justified by the fresh reputational harm adduced by the subsequent republication – reaching a different online audience and damaging personal dignity afresh, when the initial publication may have been long forgotten. For these reasons, it is also argued that republication by the same publisher of the statement online should also warrant a finding that this is materially different, and s 8 disapplied. There may be some prima facie support for this approach in s 8(5)(b) itself, which notes that 'extent' of publication is relevant to establishing whether the publication is materially different.[154]

d. A mitigating factor: s 32A of the Limitation Act 1980

There is one mitigating factor that may work to ease concerned claimants in a *republication online over a year later* scenario, albeit

---

[153] Defamation Act 2013.
[154] Ibid.

in a narrow category of cases. In *Denman*, Sir David Eady observed that there is still a way to avoid the application of s 8's limitation period, even if the statement that is republished is substantially the same. Sir Eady noted that by using s 32A Limitation Act 1980 a judge can hold that despite s 8's limitation period, it is still 'equitable' for the case to proceed.[155] However, this is entirely at the discretion of the court and for this workaround to apply circumstances have to be of an 'exceptional nature'.[156] In *Denman*, the court observed that the leave obtained under s 32A is only granted in a narrow set of circumstances: 'The court must have regard to any prejudice that would be caused to either side. It has been long recognised that the exercise of that discretionary jurisdiction is exceptional because, for reasons of public policy, time is treated as being of the essence in the defamation context.'[157]

In other words, judges will be slow to grant leave under s 32A of the Limitation Act 1980, unless there is a compelling or unusual reason why there has been a delay in bringing proceedings. The court will not be persuaded by those who want to 're-fight old battles'.[158] From the text of 32A itself, it is clear that the court is expected to undertake a delicate balancing exercise between the rights of claimants and defendants and assess to what extent it will cause them prejudice in disapplying the limitation period.[159] In *Hemming v Poulton*, the High Court stated that 'it is recognised that a court should be hesitant to exercise its discretion under s.32A'.[160] This is because the purpose of a libel action, according to the court,

---

[155] *Denman v Associated Newspapers Ltd* [2016] EWHC 2819 (QB) [8].

[156] Ibid.

[157] Ibid [7]. Also see: *Steedman v BBC* [2001] EWCA Civ 1534, *Austin v Newcastle Chronicle and Journal Ltd* [2001] EWCA Civ 834, *Bewry v Reed Elsevier* [2015] 1 WLR 2565 [5]–[8].

[158] *Denman v Associated Newspapers* (n 155) [10].

[159] Section 32A (1)(a) and (b) Limitation Act 1980.

[160] *Hemming v Poulton* [2023] EWHC 3001 (KB) [131].

is to achieve swift justice.[161] It is hard to see how this reason would be served by barring a claim (which would deliver no justice whatsoever). More charitably, courts are in the difficult position of considering allowing a needy claimant's action to proceed, while at the same time attempting not to undermine the will of parliament with s 8. The final point, then, is that this exception to the rule of s 8 will only be applicable in a narrow set of circumstances. This may not give much cause for hope to claimants with respect to a *republication online over a year later* scenario, as the balancing exercise in s 32A is a difficult one to meet and looks to only disapply s 8 in rare eventualities.

IV. Concluding remarks for Part I

Part I of this chapter has focused on two developments in libel reform introduced by the Defamation Act 2013: the introduction of the serious harm threshold in s 1 of the Act and the single publication rule in s 8. The serious harm threshold has quite significantly raised the bar for claimants generally, with the evidentiary route for proving the threshold has been met still the most likely way s 1 can be satisfied. Claimants litigating in a *defamation by social media* scenario may find the threshold particularly difficult to meet, due to these evidentiary requirements and the struggle of otherwise making out an inferential case. The courts' preoccupation with engagement statistics on social media has not served to help matters as data is not always reliable and can obfuscate more pertinent issues. Some members of the judiciary also seem to have a tacit mistrust of social media communication, with the preordained belief that statements posted on social media may be inherently less serious; once again making meeting this threshold harder. In the *republication online over a year later* scenario, claimants are also met with serious hindrances to their claim. Unless they can establish

---

[161] Ibid.

that the second defamatory publication in question is materially different from the first publication by the same publisher, then the claim will be barred as it is outside s 8's statutory limitation period of one year. It is as yet unclear exactly how different two publications must be in order not to be deemed substantially the same; more guidance from an authoritative court is awaited. Raising the threshold claimants must meet to bring an action, and limiting the time they have to do it, are both draconian ways to reduce the ability of claimants to bring actions in defamation, be these in respect to statements posted on or offline. Both of these developments have created a 'perfect storm' for claimants seeking redress for online defamation. It is now harder than ever to bring an action, at a time when the unbridled dissemination abilities of the internet can communicate defamatory content worldwide anytime, anywhere and at a click of a button.

★★★

Part II: Liability of host websites and defamation by an AI tool

Part I of this chapter focused on two *legal* developments in the Defamation Act 2013 reform that have made bringing an action in online defamation more challenging. Part II will consider two *technological* phenomena of online defamation that may be present in an action. The first instance that will be considered is when a defamatory post is published by a third party onto a 'host' website – can or should action be taken against that website? Many websites now have capabilities for users to leave comments under posts or articles and other capabilities for users to publicly interact with one another, such as virtual worlds. Newspaper websites, such as the *Mail Online*, often have active comment sections.[162] Responding to the posts of

---

[162] www.dailymail.co.uk/home/index.html accessed 1 December 2024. At the time of writing, the *Mail Online* had 22.4 million 'followers' on Facebook.

others is a key functionality of social media websites such as X, while virtual worlds can now be entered and used as conduits to disseminate defamatory information.[163] However, it may not always be possible or desirable to bring an action against a third party who has posted a comment. It will be discussed here whether a claimant in the *third-party poster* scenario can bring an action instead against the website operator (or host) themselves. The second phenomenon that will be considered is the burgeoning ability for individuals to be defamed by an AI program. As discussed in Chapter 1, the technological capabilities of the internet have advanced at a staggering pace. It is now entirely possible that a program powered by AI can communicate defamatory statements about another person, either directly to a user or posted to the internet more widely. AI regularly 'hallucinates' and creates false information about living people when responding to text prompts. This section will consider who should be actioned against by a claimant in such an eventuality. This is the *defamation by AI tool* scenario. Both of these technological issues as present in an action will have a pivotal impact on the success of a claim and how it is assessed.

I. The defence for operators of websites under s 5 Defamation Act 2013

a. A new defence

In the *third-party poster* scenario, claimants are seeking redress against a defamatory statement that has been posted to a website by a third party who is potentially anonymous or difficult to contact. Section 5 of the Defamation Act 2013 gives a new defence to website operators in these circumstances, in the

---

[163] See, for example, the Metaverse: Meta, 'What is the Metaverse?' https://about.meta.com/uk/what-is-the-metaverse/ accessed 1 December 2024.

event that they may be claimed against instead. The defence is applicable if the operators did not post that defamatory material themselves and complied with the annexed statutory regulations.[164] Section 5 states:

> (2) It is a defence for the operator to show that it was not the operator who posted the statement on the website.[165]
>
> (3) The defence is defeated if the claimant shows that ...
>
>   (b) the claimant gave the operator a notice of complaint in relation to the statement, and
>
>   (c) the operator failed to respond to the notice of complaint in accordance with any provision contained in regulations.[166]

In other words, in order for a website operator to rely on the defence against an action from a claimant, in the *third-party poster* scenario they must show that they followed the procedure outlined by the statutory instrument annexed to s 5.[167] The statutory instrument observes that with 48 hours of a notice from a prospective claimant concerning (potentially) defamatory content posted on the website,[168] the web host must send notice of that complaint to the third-party poster.[169] An explanation should also be sent to the poster that the statement will be removed from the website,[170] unless there is a response in writing to protesting the contrary by the end of

---

[164] The Defamation (Operators of Websites) Regulations 2013, Statutory Instrument No 3028 www.legislation.gov.uk/uksi/2013/3028/contents/made accessed 1 December 2024.
[165] Sections 5(2) Defamation Act 2013.
[166] Sections 5(3)(b) and (c) of the Defamation Act 2013.
[167] The Defamation (Operators of Websites) Regulations (n 164).
[168] Ibid Schedule 2(1).
[169] Ibid Schedule 2(1)(a).
[170] Ibid Schedule 2(1)(b).

the fifth day after the notification is sent.[171] If the poster does not wish for the content to be removed they must provide their full name and address,[172] so that they can be actioned against as an individual in defamation by the prospective claimant. If the third-party poster fails to respond by the end of the fifth day, 48 hours later the statement complained of must be removed from the website by the host.[173]

It is argued that this is one of the few examples of good practice in the 2013 Act, which seeks to balance the interests of both those who have been defamed online on the one hand and, on the other, the expression rights and economic interests of host websites and users. It allows for a potentially swift remedy for claimants in the form of the information's removal from a website at the end of the fifth day, absent of any contrary protestations from the poster (and the provision of their contact details). In the event a third-party poster objects to the removal of the statement, they need only request this and provide their details, such that an action can be brought against them individually in defamation – and have their day in court. This means that the statement remains on the website in this interim period. Interestingly, much like s 8 of the Defamation Act 2013 and the US single publication rule, there is a counterpart US law that mirrors the s 5 defence. Section 230 of the Communications Decency Act 1996 in America states that 'no provider or user of an interactive computer service shall be treated as the publisher or speaker of any information provided by another information content provider'.[174]

---

[171] Ibid Schedule 2(1)(b)(i).
[172] Ibid Schedule 2(2)(b)(i) and (ii).
[173] Ibid Schedule 5(1) and (2)(a).
[174] Communications Decency Act of 1996, 47 USC § 230 (2016) and Dallin Albright, 'Do androids defame with actual malice? Libel in the world of automated journalism' (2023) 75 *Federal Communications Law Journal* 103, 108.

b. Potential issues

Section 5 largely succeeds in treading a narrow line between competing rights, but it too has imperfections. Given the unlimited defamatory potential of the internet and the rise in defamation on social media and other websites, it was unwise of the section to adopt the default position that if a statement's removal is contested, it remains visible on the host website while a claimant brings an action against the third-party poster. This does nothing to readdress the clear imbalance in favour of Article 10 ECHR rights in the digital age, or to lessen the effect of the 2013 Act reform that prioritizes expression at the expense of reputation. With every day the potentially defamatory statement remains online, the more harm to personal dignity and one's self-perception can be rendered,[175] as the statement may continue to reach new audiences – or could even be subject to an upwards trend and 'go viral' and reach hundreds of thousands of new readers.[176] This position is also out of step with the privacy tort of misuse of private information in England and Wales. In actions for misuse of private information, a claimant can apply to a court to have an interim injunction that prohibits disclosure of the complained-of material pending trial.[177] Although these applications are at the discretion of the court (and are not always successful), long-standing common law rules show that obtaining a comparable interim injunction in a defamation case is not possible. This divergence of approach

---

[175] See Chapter 2.

[176] Reaching tens of thousands of readers in a short space of time is considered 'going viral' on X. See 'How many views is viral?' (*Fourthwall*, 6 March 2024) https://fourthwall.com/blog/how-many-views-is-viral accessed 1 December 2024.

[177] For the current test for such an order, see *Cream Holdings Ltd v Banerjee and Others* [2005] 1 AC 253 [22] and *NPV v QEL and ZED* [2018] EWHC 703 (QB).

is further compounded by s 5's position that complained-of posts must remain visible, pending trial – which once again disadvantages personality interests.

At just over a decade old, the Defamation Act 2013 is still considered 'new' in the context of English defamation law. As such, academics and practitioners alike await guidance about many of the new defence's parameters. One issue that remains unclear is if the defence will be considered applicable to large social media websites such as Facebook, X, YouTube, Instagram and virtual online worlds such as the Metaverse. The court in *Goldsmith v Bissett Powell* observed 'there is no authority that I am aware of relating to Facebook administrators and whether they fall within s 5'.[178] In a *third-party poster* scenario, a claimant may find that a defamatory post has been published to a public network on Facebook or the Metaverse, but the poster themselves is not directly contactable to serve an action against. They may operate their posting account under a pseudonym, giving out no other details on the given social media site, and remain unresponsive to direct messages from the person defamed. If this is the case, it is argued here that this defence *should* be applicable to a large social media website or virtual world host. This would incentivize a large platform such as Facebook or its parent company Meta to directly contact a poster as per the statutory instrument on receipt of a complaint, which will more likely engender a response due to the perceived power imbalance between a poster and a large conglomerate. Ultimately, this will lead to the defamatory statement's removal or sufficient contact details of the third-party poster being passed on to the claimant so an action can be brought directly. This at the very least is a clear route to some potential redress in court on the part of a claimant.

---

[178] *Goldsmith v Bissett-Powell* (n 52) [169].

c. Approach of the Strasbourg Court

To date, there have been two high-profile decisions at the European Court of Human Rights (ECtHR) which consider host website liability for third-party comments posted to online news portals: *Delfi* and *Magyar*.[179] The point that arises from both Strasbourg cases, at least implicitly, is that online content providers or 'hosts' can be subject to civil liability for infringement of personality rights through comments posted by others.[180] These provide an interesting point of comparison for the s 5 defence for web hosts, in terms of how far the defence extends and what sort of responsibilities the English courts in future may impose on website providers in relation to defamatory material posted by others to their sites. As yet there is little case law on the s 5 defence, but it seems likely in future that the precise scope of the defence will be tested in courts, perhaps by large web operators who wish to argue the defence is applicable. There is much academics and practitioners do not know about the s 5 defence, which must be dictated by the passage of the common law. In *Delfi*, Strasbourg's Grand Chamber upheld the earlier First Section's judgment that the Estonian national courts' decision to hold an internet news portal liable for offensive comments made under an article by third parties was *not* a violation of Article 10 ECHR.[181] In *Magyar*, a year later, the opposite finding was reached: the Hungarian courts, in holding a regulatory body and a news portal liable for third-party defamatory comments posted by others to the news website, *were* in violation of the right to freedom of expression.[182] Although at first glance

---

[179] *Delfi AS v Estonia* App no 64569/09 (16 June 2015). *Magyar Tartalomszolgaltatok Egyesulete v Hungary* App no 22947/13 (2 February 2016).

[180] Also see Andras Koltay, *New Media and Freedom of Expression* (Hart 2019) ch 6.

[181] *Delfi AS v Estonia* (n 179) [162].

[182] *Magyar v Hungary* (n 179) [91ff].

these decisions may seem contradictory, a closer examination reveals this is not the case. The deciding factors of finding no violation (in *Delfi*'s case) and the contrary finding in *Magyar* were rooted in the degree of balancing domestic courts had conducted with a view to assessing the competing Article 8 rights of those defamed or threatened by the comments on the one hand, and the rights of internet service providers, website hosts and internet users more broadly under Article 10 on the other. Perhaps the most important aspect of both decisions are the balancing factors the ECtHR expounded in *Delfi* – and reused in *Magyar* – in order to guide Article 8 and 10 balancing in such a situation. These factors could provide a framework for English courts to employ (as at the very least, a starting point) when adjudicating future decisions on the scope or applicability of the s 5 defence.

By way of background, *Delfi v Estonia* was handed down by the Grand Chamber in 2015,[183] on appeal from the First Section decision in 2013.[184] The matter concerned an online news website named Delfi, a prolific Eastern European news site with a wide readership.[185] It was straightforward for third parties to add comments under a news article on Delfi's platform. People could choose their own name or a pseudonym, the provision of an email address was not essential and comments were uploaded by default.[186] As such, comparatively little oversight by Delfi was necessary for comments to appear under news stories published on the website. The few safeguards Delfi did have in place were that certain obscene words were filtered and there was a notice-and-takedown mechanism for 'hate' comments,[187] encompassing comments or words of the most

---

[183] *Delfi AS v Estonia* [2015] (n 179).
[184] *Delfi AS v Estonia* App no 64569/09 (ECHR, 10 October 2013).
[185] Ibid [7].
[186] Ibid [8].
[187] Ibid [9].

offensive kind.[188] The matter at issue concerned an article Delfi had posted about a shipping company which it claimed had quashed plans for an ice road in Estonia.[189] Twenty third-party comments posted under the article personally attacked person 'L', a significant shareholder at the company,[190] using threatening and abusive language.[191] The national courts in Estonia found that Delfi was a publisher of the third-party posts and damages were awarded.[192] Importantly, the Grand Chamber decision in *Delfi* upheld a number of balancing factors articulated by the earlier 2013 decision in finding Article 10 had not been infringed.[193] The court went on to apply these factors to the matters at hand.

Firstly, the Grand Chamber considered the factor of the *context of the comments*. Under this headline, the court deemed it relevant that Delfi had control over the comment section on its website and was therefore in a position to moderate content uploaded by others.[194] It was deemed important that Delfi was a popular website that often attracted many comments, and that more comments meant more website traffic and therefore more advertising revenue for Delfi's benefit.[195] Delfi as a website was involved in content moderation, had regulations for third-party comments and did not play the role of a merely passive intermediary.[196] Secondly, the Grand Chamber considered the factor of *liability for authors of the comments*. Under this factor, it was seen relevant that it was difficult to bring an action against

---

[188] Although these filters were later deemed ineffective in *Delfi AS v Estonia* [2015] (n 179) [156].
[189] *Delfi AS v Estonia* [2013] (n 184) [12].
[190] Ibid [14].
[191] Ibid [13].
[192] *Delfi AS v Estonia* [2015] [26].
[193] Ibid [64] and *Delfi AS v Estonia* [2013] (n 184) [86].
[194] *Delfi AS v Estonia* [2015] [144].
[195] Ibid.
[196] Ibid.

the authors of the comments themselves due to the anonymous nature of the internet.[197] Therefore, actioning against Delfi was seen as a legitimate and necessary alternative. The third and perhaps most important factor applied was *measures taken by applicant company*. The thread in question would have likely drawn the attention of Delfi staff, as the comment section was unusually active.[198] Despite this, there was still a delay in Delfi removing the offending comments. The word filter employed as a method of offensive content moderation was regarded by the court as unfit for purpose, as offensive comments had slipped through the net, as was the notice-and-takedown policy – which the court viewed as too lengthy a process to sufficiently safeguard against hateful comments such as those at issue.[199] Finally, following the First Section, the Grand Chamber considered the factor of *consequences for the applicant company*. They found that there were no significant long-term negative effects for Delfi as a result of the Estonian courts' decision, as a fine was issued but Delfi did not in fact need to change its business model in order to accommodate the ruling. Damages for non-pecuniary loss had not been awarded and, as such, the remedies enforced were far from draconian.[200] An important point to emphasize regarding *Delfi* is that the comments complained of amounted to hate speech,[201] and were 'low-value' speech,[202] and for this reason, the decision was not as controversial as some have attempted to claim.[203] While some defamatory statements may tread the line of hate

---

[197] Ibid [147].

[198] Ibid [152]–[153].

[199] Ibid [156]–[159].

[200] Ibid [160].

[201] Ibid [159].

[202] In the form of insults and threats.

[203] Lorna Woods, 'The *Delfi AS v Estonia* judgment explained' (*LSE Media Policy Project Blog*, 16 June 2015) https://blogs.lse.ac.uk/mediapolicyproject/2015/06/16/the-delfi-as-vs-estonia-judgement-explained/ accessed 2 September 2019, and Neville Cox, '*Delfi AS v Estonia*: The liability of

speech, many reputationally damaging statements that are actionable under English law would not. The result of the hateful nature of the comments in *Delfi* was that the failure to remove the comments quickly was seen by the court as particularly egregious. As a result of the application of these factors, the court concurred with the First Section's 2013 finding that Article 10 had not been violated.

This method of analysis was followed in the decision of *Magyar* a year later. Here, the court found that the Hungarian national courts had violated freedom of expression by finding a regulatory body of internet service providers and a news portal liable for third-party comments, due to errors in balancing rights conducted by the Hungarian courts.[204] In finding whether an appropriate balance had been struck between Article 8 and Article 10, the Strasbourg Court utilized each of the balancing factors listed by *Delfi* in order to guide their analysis.[205] In *Magyar* the court found that the article which generated the third-party comments in question was on an important matter of public interest (factor: *context in which the comments were posted*).[206] The court also found that it made sense in this case to find those who had made the comments themselves legally responsible according to the *liability for authors of the comments* criterion.[207] Additionally, the website in *Magyar* had removed the comments as soon as it was told about them (*measures taken by applicant website*),[208] therefore acting more swiftly than Delfi. In terms of the *consequences* factor, the court observed in *Magyar* that the claimant's reputation had already

---

secondary internet publishers for violation of reputational rights under the European Convention on Human Rights' (2014) 77(4) *Modern Law Review* 619.

[204] *Magyar v Hungary* (n 179) [2].
[205] Ibid [63]–[71].
[206] Ibid [72].
[207] Ibid [78].
[208] Ibid [80].

been significantly damaged in light of other comments not complained of and that a threshold of seriousness had not been applied by domestic courts when examining the case.[209] In all senses, the facts of the case in *Magyar* were weaker according to the balancing factors articulated by the court than those in *Delfi*. The judgment in *Magyar* is a demonstration of the breadth and flexibility of the *Delfi* factors and how they can be applied to different facts to reach diametrically opposed conclusions. *Magyar* is also useful as a further example of application of the *Delfi* factors in the event that English courts seek to rely on them for reference when adjudicating a future s 5 dispute. The *consequences* of the decision appear to be particularly important from the perspective of the ECtHR (for both claimants and defendants), as do the *nature and severity* of the comments and the likelihood of it being *realistically possible* to bring an action against third-party posters themselves. Finally, it should be noted that the ECtHR (somewhat controversially) went yet further in the case of *Sanchez v France* in 2023, when the Grand Chamber found that Article 10 ECHR had *not* been violated by the French courts imposing a criminal sanction on Mr Sanchez, a local councillor, after he did not remove hate speech from his Facebook page despite it being posted there by third parties.[210] In the case, the relevant French laws were found to purse the legitimate aims of the reputation of others, as well as the prevention of crime.[211] This decision may, however, be explained with reference to the particular facts of the case. *Sanchez* concerned hateful Islamophobic comments posted to a Mr Sanchez's Facebook wall during election time, when Mr Sanchez himself – already involved in local politics – was running for parliamentary election.[212]

---

[209] Ibid [85].
[210] *Sanchez v France* App 45581/15 (15 May 2023) [3].
[211] Ibid [144].
[212] Ibid [11] and [14ff].

The crime in France he was convicted for was the incitement of violence or hatred on the grounds of religion.[213] The facts of the case are more aligned to hate speech rather than falling clearly into the remit of defamation law, perhaps even more so than in the case of *Delfi* itself (where certain comments were also found to be threatening and hateful, therefore also crossing the line into hate speech).[214] In making its finding of no violation, the ECtHR noted it relevant that Mr Sanchez was involved in politics,[215] the court finding that for politicians, 'when expressing themselves in public, to avoid comments that might foster intolerance'[216] and to 'foster the exclusion of foreigners constitutes a fundamental attack on individual rights, and everyone – politicians included – should exercise particular caution in discussing such matters'.[217] In the decision, *Delfi*'s precedent was considered and the factors discussed there were applied.[218] *Context of the comments* was considered (including their nature),[219] the *political context* was also considered as well as *specific applicant liability for third-party comments*.[220] *Steps taken* by Sanchez were also examined,[221] as well as the *possibility of holding the authors liable*,[222] and the *consequences* of the domestic decision.[223] The *Delfi* criteria for host liability is therefore still going strong and has shown through *Sanchez* that it can be applied to render liability for *private individuals* who can also seen as web hosts (in this case, Mr Sanchez and his Facebook

---

[213] Ibid [3].

[214] Ibid: Part B of the Grand Chamber's decision that discusses hate speech specifically [60ff].

[215] *Sanchez v France* (n 210) [149]–[150].

[216] Ibid [150]

[217] Ibid.

[218] Ibid [169ff].

[219] Ibid [169].

[220] Ibid [179].

[221] Ibid [190].

[222] Ibid [202].

[223] Ibid [205].

wall), as well as large conglomerates. It is important, however, to note that the facts of *Sanchez*, given the political context and nature of the comments, were particularly egregious.

Interestingly, the Grand Chamber's decision in *Delfi* differentiates online news portals from social media websites on the basis that social media sites do not generate their own content.[224] It is respectfully submitted here that this distinction is outdated and out of touch with the practical operation of social media websites today. Many social media sites mix user-generated posts and posts generated by the host platform, either by company employees themselves or by outsourcing to freelance content creators. An example of such content would be 'YouTube Rewind', which is the tradition of YouTube itself releasing a video recapping memorable yearly events through a YouTube narrative, largely by employing the talents of independent creators on the site to star in the video itself.[225] Similarly, Facebook now embeds articles from other websites in its landing page and displays advertisements.[226] With the introduction of rapidly evolving AI programs across the internet, the distinction between social media, virtual worlds, news portals and other types of website on which users can leave comments is set to become increasingly blurred. For these reasons, it is argued here that as helpful as the laundry list of factors laid out in *Delfi* (and followed by *Magyar*) may be, they provide far from all the answers to disputes that are yet to come about the scope and application of the s 5 defence. In any event, for these reasons, alongside those articulated earlier, it is argued here that the s 5 defence should be operable not only with regard to the likes of news portals but also social media websites such as

---

[224] *Delfi AS v Estonia* [2015] [112] and [116].
[225] See, for example, 'YouTube Rewind 2018: Everyone controls Rewind' www.youtube.com/watch?v=YbJOTdZBX1g accessed 9 January 2025.
[226] Facebook, 'Branded content, "Overview"' www.facebook.com/facebookmedia/get-started/branded-content accessed 23 April 2018.

X, YouTube, Facebook, Instagram and, by extension, virtual worlds (which operate as wider-scale social media sites) where users can interact and disseminate defamatory information. Applicability of the s 5 defence to these types of sites provides a clear incentive for large website operators to act swiftly to provide third-party poster contact information so that they can be individually actioned against in defamation – or else remove the offending post in question. Helpfully, the more recent case of *Sanchez* at the Grand Chamber has in fact shown the willingness of the Strasbourg Court to extend *Delfi* principles to social media websites (Facebook), to at least render private-individual 'hosts' liable for third-party comments.[227]

II. Defamation by an AI tool

a. A rising threat

While AI begins to demonstrate the staggering scale of its capabilities throughout the world,[228] many questions about online libel remain unanswered. The challenge of identifying an appropriate defendant to bring an action against in the *defamation by AI tool* scenario is complex. It seems unclear as yet whether existing legal frameworks in England and Wales can effectively tackle such an eventuality. It should be noted at this stage that this book is primarily concerned with generative AI and its defamatory capabilities. There are undoubtedly pressing problems with analytical AI tools and

---

[227] *Sanchez* (n 210).

[228] For example, on the day of writing, OpenAI made a video generator publicly accessible. See Dara Kerr, 'OpenAI makes AI video generator Sora publicly available in US' *The Guardian* (9 December 2024) www.theguardian.com/technology/2024/dec/09/openai-ai-video-generator-sora-publicly-available accessed 10 December 2024.

their concerning tendency towards bias and discrimination[229] – but this is outside the argument advanced in this work. The rapid advancement of AI and its acceptance in everyday life shows no sign of halting. Respected broadsheet newspapers, such as *The Guardian* and, in the US, *The Washington Post*, have already trialled AI-written articles.[230] However, it is obvious that without rigorous oversight, fully automated production of AI news pieces could lead to false information presented as fact.[231] As AI programs are primarily used, downloaded and accessed through the internet, the public's increased reliance on the internet compounds the implications for personal dignity when one is defamed online in the *defamation by AI tool* scenario.[232] As noted in Chapter 1, the attention span of the 'digital generation' has reduced – and spreading disinformation online may be particularly effective in part due to short durations of engagement,[233] where individuals accessing the defamatory content do not have time to question its accuracy. Volokh observes that companies which create AI programs regularly promote their programs as reliable in order to ensure they are marketable; it therefore follows that this invites legal responsibility when users believe untrue, defamatory claims produced by that AI system.[234] In light of this, it is not a valid defence for companies that create AI programs to then argue later at trial that information was never intended to be completely accurate, or held out to be so.[235]

---

[229] See, for example, Nima Kordzadeh and Maryam Ghasemaghaei, 'Algorithmic bias: Review, synthesis, and future research directions' (2022) 31(3) *European Journal of Information Systems* 388.
[230] Albright (n 174) 104.
[231] Ibid 109.
[232] Ibid 110.
[233] Ibid.
[234] Eugene Volokh, 'Large libel models? Liability for AI output' (2023) 3 *Journal of Free Speech Law* 489, 498.
[235] Ibid 499.

Indeed, English defamation law would not require everyone who read an AI program's defamatory statement to believe it to be true; rather, it is instead a test of what the 'reasonable reader' believed.[236] The defamatory potential of generative AI systems is also concerning because of their power to sway thought through their large outreach online.[237] As Albright observes, 'dissemination follows naturally' on social media.[238]

There are many different types of AI system, with varying levels of human involvement. So-called semi-autonomous production allows the AI system room to generate its own content more freely than other types of production and to publish information without oversight. As a result, this type of AI program can lead to an increased likelihood of defamatory content being generated. This type of program is also seen as particularly valuable in industry, as it has the potential to generate content that feels more 'natural', 'human' and ultimately convincing – with less costs for overheads before publishing.[239] The most popular type of AI program currently is 'a pretrained generative model on the whole internet', where input data is 'only lightly curated'.[240] Examples of such systems are predictive text models like ChatGPT-2 and 3.[241] Predictive text models often do not 'opt-out' of answering user-prompted questions and instead may fabricate information in order to (one can only assume) satisfy the end-user.[242] Language models

---

[236] Ibid.

[237] Inyoung Cheong, Aylin Caliskan and Tadayoshi Kohno, 'Safeguarding human values: Rethinking US law for generative AI's societal impacts' (2024) 5 *AI and Ethics* 1433 https://doi.org/10.1007/s43681-024-00451-4 accessed 10 December 2024.

[238] Albright (n 174) 110.

[239] Ibid 108.

[240] Peter Henderson, Tatsunori Hashimoto and Mark Lemley, 'Where's the liability in harmful AI speech?' (2023) 3 *Journal of Free Speech Law* 589, 620–2, 602, and Volokh (n 234).

[241] Ibid Henderson (n 240).

[242] Ibid 603.

can also be influenced by training websites that contain untrue, hateful or offensive speech that companies have failed to weed out at an earlier stage.[243] As Cheong, Caliskan and Kohno have observed, error testing is expensive, lengthy and difficult to resource, particularly for small companies.[244]

b. The nature of the threat

The prevailing facet of generative AI that is leading it to publish potentially defamatory content is the phenomena of AI 'hallucinating'. In other words, AI is regularly observed creating false information in response to prompts – including that which concerns other people – and cannot be traced back to input data.[245] It is as yet unclear how or why AI programs do this, although it is a disturbingly common occurrence. This false material is then presented as fact, often confidently, to the AI tool user – and it is impossible prima facie to know this has occurred. This appears to be the case for many large language models (LLMs).[246] Through his own usage of the systems, Volokh has noted that they 'seem to routinely erroneously produce false and defamatory statements'.[247] For some reason, these hallucinations have the proclivity to be reputationally damaging and of a particularly destructive nature to personal dignity. On testing, ChatGPT for example regularly accuses people of crimes they have not committed.[248] There is currently a libel suit in progress against OpenAI as well as a claim open against search engine Bing, which uses AI program ChatGPT 4, which falsely claimed that a professor was a convicted criminal (after the program confused the professor for a known

---

[243] Ibid 603–4.
[244] Cheong, Caliskan and Kohno (n 237) 6.
[245] Henderson, Hashimoto and Lemley (n 240) 591.
[246] Volokh (n 234) 492.
[247] Ibid.
[248] Henderson, Hashimoto and Lemley (n 240) 591.

terrorist with a similar name).²⁴⁹ Quotations purportedly from others communicated to users by AI models are regularly incorrect or completely fabricated.²⁵⁰ Such hallucinations do not appear to be attributable to 'bad inputs': it is rather 'the way large language models work'.²⁵¹ Early research suggests this may be because these models generate predicted text, which leads to the AI system falsifying information in order to provide an answer to a question prompt in the event the program is not able to (honestly) answer the question.²⁵² False statements such as these are presented conclusively as accurate information by these language models.²⁵³ Cheong, Caliskan and Kohno have even noted that AI can be 'opinionated' – thereby unknowingly influencing a user to believe that every answer generated is implicitly correct.²⁵⁴ As many individuals have moved to consuming their news through social media rather than traditional newspapers, communication channels have now changed and AI is looking poised to dominate online social media in the near future.²⁵⁵ The hallucination problem is so rife that AI language models have been seen to generate defamatory outputs even to non-malicious questions about an individual.²⁵⁶ This defamation problem is only likely to increase in significance as people across the globe begin to rely on AI tools and implicitly believe the information generated by these systems.²⁵⁷

These practical threats are underscored by the current lack of legislative or adequate common law control over AI

---

[249] Volokh (n 234) 492.
[250] Ibid 529.
[251] Henderson, Hashimoto and Lemley (n 240) 592.
[252] Ibid.
[253] Ibid.
[254] Cheong, Caliskan and Kohno (n 237) 3.
[255] Albright (n 174) 122–3.
[256] Henderson, Hashimoto and Lemley (n 240) 596.
[257] Volokh (n 234) 493.

developments on a significant scale. The most comprehensive piece of legislation to date concerning AI worldwide is the European Union's recent and pioneering 'AI Act', although this is not UK law after 'Brexit' in 2020. Despite the scale of AI's insurgence into everyday lives online, the UK appears reticent to apply strict regulation to this online space, regardless of the obvious threats of AI programs to personality interests and human rights.[258] It is not clear if this legal reticence is due to a lack of understanding, fears about quashing economic or creative benefits, or instead a concern over the complexity of the legal task involved. Compounding the problem, there seems to be little appetite on the part of AI program manufacturers to prioritize fixing the problem of AI-generated defamation, despite its prevalence.[259]

c. Who should be responsible for an AI tool's defamatory speech?

It is argued here that there is a clear and pressing need for the law to accommodate claims in defamation when an individual is defamed by an AI program and then these defamatory statements are published – in other words, communicated[260] – to another individual. This is for two reasons, outlined earlier. One is because this is a very real threat, as demonstrated by the propensity of LLMs to defame, shown through their proclivity to hallucinate. The other is that defamatory imputations spread in this way can cause very real harm for the individuals concerned, as information is now regularly consumed through the medium of the internet, with a degree of trust extended to AI programs that are marketed as reputable. Despite legislative

---

[258] Cheong, Caliskan and Kohno (n 237) 2.

[259] Volokh (n 234) 493.

[260] English law has made clear that publication, even to only one person (outside the claimant themselves), will be sufficient publication, or as Horsey and Rackley term it, 'communication', in the law. See Kirsty Horsey and Erika Rackley, *Tort Law* (7th edn, OUP 2021) 504.

reticence, calls for legal involvement in this area are becoming louder. Albright has argued that a 'stricter duty' in US law should apply to those who use an AI device to defame others, in order to tackle burgeoning risks.[261] Due to the increased possibilities the internet provides to defame, aided by AI programs, the rate at which defamatory information can be generated and communicated online is unfathomable. It is crucial, then, that there are routes for redress in defamation against both third-party publishers of that information but also AI program manufacturers. For example, a third-party publisher may be a living individual who uses an AI program to generate defamatory content; the program then publishes it further afield, in a *defamation by AI tool* scenario. A manufacturer would be the company responsible for designing, programming, training and putting the AI program that has generated that defamatory content to market. Of course, an AI program itself 'publishes' or sufficiently communicates the defamatory statement when it answers a text prompt from a human user and defames another individual. The requirement of publication in English defamation law has always been satisfied by one-to-one communication, outside of (for example) a call between a claimant and defendant themselves.[262] It is not currently legally practicable to bring a claim against an AI tool itself in the English jurisdiction – firstly, because such a tool does not have a separate legal personality in the eyes of English law, unlike companies;[263] and secondly, because it would not

---

[261] Albright (n 174) 105.

[262] Henderson, Hashimoto and Lemley (n 240) 635–6; Volokh (n 234) 504; and Horsey and Rackley (n 260) 504.

[263] Although the advantages of effectively 'incorporating' AI and therefore giving it legal personality are being mooted. See, for example, James Russell, 'Artificial intelligence and separate legal personality' (*Inside Tech Law: Norton Rose Fulbright*, 12 November 2019) www.insidetechlaw.com/blog/2019/11/artificial-intelligence-and-separate-legal-personality accessed 18 December 2024; and Visa AJ Kurki, 'The legal personhood of artificial intelligences' in *A Theory of Legal Personhood* (OUP 2019) ch 6.

independently have the funds to support any compensation awarded in a successful claim. Website hosts that merely host defamatory content generated by a third party (including an AI program) may be protected under the s 5 operators of websites defence in the Defamation Act 2013, discussed earlier in this chapter. However, this defence would likely fall away if the website itself played an active rather than passive role in disseminating defamatory information generated by AI software.[264] The defence would also fail to be operational in the event that the web hosts had been made aware of the defamatory content generated by an AI tool hosted on their website, were effectively 'on notice',[265] and yet failed to act on that information as per the statutory instrument.[266] Section 5 will not provide a defence for the manufacturer or user of an AI tool, as the type of AI program known to commonly defame is generative and therefore is creating the defamatory information itself – and not merely regurgitating or 'hosting' information from elsewhere on the internet. Similarly, the US defence in s 230(c)(1) of the Communications Decency Act that protects those behind computer services from liability in defamation (in the event that the information had been provided by another content provider), which includes social media and search engines, is not thought to extend to generative AI systems.[267]

It is argued here that companies producing generative AI programs should be subject to liability in defamation for defamatory outputs of such tools. In addition to the points mentioned, there are two further reasons for this liability regime. Firstly, there may be a lack of recourse for claimants

---

[264] As s 5 is a defence for a web host who has *not* posted the statement complained of, as stipulated in s 5(2) Defamation Act 2013.

[265] For an argument to this effect in the US context, see Henderson, Hashimoto and Lemley (n 240) 647.

[266] The Defamation (Operators of Websites) Regulations (n 164).

[267] Henderson, Hashimoto and Lemley (n 240) 620–2 and Volokh (n 234) 494.

in terms of who else to sue – in the event that a third party has communicated information generated using an AI tool, but is not contactable. Secondly, an AI program itself is not currently able to be claimed against in English law, due to the abovementioned reasons of lack of separate legal personality and funds. Holding AI software *manufacturers* as accountable instead offers security for claimants, as such companies may have 'deep pockets' and are therefore well positioned to compensate claimants for the affront to personal dignity caused. Holding manufacturers as liable is also beneficial as they will likely have the power and influence to amend AI programs in the future, to discourage defamatory statements being generated. Indeed, Henderson, Hashimoto and Lemley have argued that holding manufacturers accountable provides a valuable incentive for them to improve the offering that they provide in a way which is beneficial for society at large.[268] If more informational safeguards are incorporated into an AI program, the less likely it is to generate harmful defamatory content in the future. This can be done through supporting programs with more rigorously curated input data, the inclusion of more checks and balances into the software and an increased amount of human testing to minimize hallucinations.[269] Cheong, Caliskan and Kohno have observed that there are insufficient 'market incentives' at present to persuade developers to produce higher-quality AI programs designed with limiting defamation in mind. This is because 'profit incentives do not automatically encourage robust safety efforts'.[270] English courts finding AI program manufacturers accountable in the *defamation by AI tool* scenario would go some way to encourage best practices in the industry. Finally, the famed English tort law policy argument of 'floodgates', or the courts wishing to safeguard

---

[268] Henderson, Hashimoto and Lemley (n 240) 636–7.
[269] Ibid 648–9.
[270] Cheong, Caliskan and Kohno (n 237) 6.

against uncontrolled liability, is not sufficiently engaged here as to cause the judiciary to feel there is any pressing concern in extending the law in this way. As has been argued in the previous chapter, English defamation law is already difficult to successfully argue as a claimant in the digital age – it has many hurdles, such as the serious harm threshold, reference to the claimant and publication itself, and a plethora of defences that a defendant could potentially rely on. Claims against defendant manufacturer companies would be limited by all of the abovementioned factors and therefore development of the law in this way would not result in an insurmountable deluge of claims.[271] This is not to say that it is beyond the capabilities of English common law to construct a method for the AI system itself to be individually responsible in defamation, in the same way that an incorporated company can be responsible in various contexts, in the realms of commercial law – rather, it is a question of practicalities, the status quo in the law and the ability of claimants to obtain a meaningful remedy.[272]

If companies producing generative AI programs are to be found capable of liability in English defamation law, the question then arises of what companies can do in order to avoid liability. One potential recourse to bolster the reliability of AI tools and ensure they do not defame is to make sure the software rigorously fact-checks itself or its sources. An appropriate standard of reliability would be whether 'the algorithm's methods meet the standards of journalistic procedure'.[273] The often limp disclaimers employed by AI companies in an attempt to shield themselves from legal responsibility should not be sufficient to stop an action against them in defamation – as a short disclaimer stating that information may not be entirely accurate is not the same as

---

[271] For this argument as broadly stated, ibid 12.
[272] For an argument relating to practicalities, see Volokh (n 234) 508.
[273] Albright (n 174) 117.

clearly stating that something is fiction or parody (ensuring that nothing is believed by an audience), particularly as AI devices are partly marketed on their reliability.[274] A practical route to make sure generative AI tools provide users with accurate information is for developers to dedicate time for the system to learn rigorously from 'human feedback' and other training modifications. This allows human developers to curate data to follow certain overarching principles.[275] This process is already engaged in to some extent by AI manufacturers. However, even if this approach is used in the development process, Henderson, Hashimoto and Lemley observe that achieving only 65 per cent accuracy is still a normal percentage to be expected,[276] which is concerningly low. To compound this problem, austere content moderation like this can sometimes *take away* from accuracy, in a confusing quirk of development.[277] There are other simpler solutions posited – such as ensuring that an AI program refuses to answer a user prompt if it cannot generate an accurate answer – which can reduce the need to AI to hallucinate in order to find one.[278] In essence, to shield itself from liability for defamation published by its AI tool, a manufacturing company should have to demonstrate that 'it has taken all reasonable measures to prevent the propagation of harmful statements',[279] in a standard reminiscent of common law negligence in the English system. Volokh has noted that this is similar to holding a newspaper editor as liable if they have not robustly fact-checked an article that then defames someone,[280] and in such a circumstance the s 4 publication on a matter of public interest defence in English law would

---

[274] Volokh (n 234) 500–2.
[275] Henderson, Hashimoto and Lemley (n 240) 612.
[276] Ibid 613.
[277] Ibid 615.
[278] Ibid 619.
[279] Cheong, Caliskan and Kohno (n 237) 10.
[280] Volokh (n 234) 522–3.

likely fall away.[281] Particular attention needs to be paid to AI devices attributing false quotations to individual, when in fact the quotations have been hallucinated by the device.[282]

It is clear from this discussion that AI tool manufacturers have a mountain to climb to ensure accuracy of AI tools. This is a costly and time-consuming process, the parameters and specifics of which are not yet fully understood. In the meantime, if AI manufacturing companies are prepared to accept the large amounts of profit generated by popular AI tools,[283] they must also accept the liability that should ultimately arise through such devices defaming third parties.

d. Deepfakes and defamation

The arguments rehearsed apply to generative AI in a comprehensive manner. Before this chapter closes, it is important to specifically address a particularly harmful branch of AI development: the rise of 'deepfakes' on the internet. A deepfake can take the form of (for example) a video that appears to be of a real person who is speaking, such as a politician – however, although the video appears to be real it is fact fictional and generated by AI. A deepfake could also take the form of a modified photograph of a person in a compromising position – perhaps sexual – or otherwise implying reputationally damaging behaviour or beliefs. This is another way that an individual can be *defamed by an AI tool*. Deepfakes are particularly damaging to a person's psychological

---

[281] As the grounds of 'reasonable belief' that publishing something was in the public interest would not be met, in s 4(1)(b) of the Defamation Act 2013.

[282] Volokh (n 234) 522–6.

[283] OpenAI was valued at $157 billion US dollars in 2024. See David Curry, 'ChatGPT revenue and usage statistics (2024)' (*Business of Apps*, 13 November 2024) www.businessofapps.com/data/chatgpt-statistics/ accessed 20 December 2024.

integrity, personal dignity and self-perception, as being exposed to a lifelike video of something they appear to be doing may even lead them to question themselves. High-quality deepfakes, many of which can be seen today due to advancements in technology, appear to be real and can be incredibly convincing. The defamatory implications of such videos are obvious and deepfake production has been something of an internet phenomenon. Deep learning is responsible for this breakthrough,[284] and the production value of deepfakes is increasing as individuals share best practises for producing deepfakes through internet message boards.[285] The AI tools that power the creation of such fakes are often open source and there are applications available to download to create deepfakes that 'require little to no coding skills'.[286] This means that the creation of deepfakes is possible by many and not limited to a class of individuals who necessarily have the technical skill or financial backing. A shocking 90 per cent of deepfakes are pornographic.[287] This means that deepfakes pose a particularly concerning threat to one's personal dignity, as when one's likeness is misused in this intimate and violating manner it is also likely to cause feelings of shame and embarrassment and have a potentially grave impact on individual reputation. The disturbing motive of creating deepfakes of real individuals depicting sex acts online is clear, as Karasavva and Noorbhai observe: 'using deepfake technology, anyone could direct their own pornographic material, casting people from their own lives'.[288] To make matters worse, accurate detection of

---

[284] Ángel Fernández Gambín, Anis Yazidi, Athanasios Vasilakos, Hårek Haugerud and Youcef Djenouri, 'Deepfakes: Current and future trends' (2024) 57(64) *Artificial Intelligence Review* 1, 1.

[285] Vasileia Karasavva and Aalia Noorbhai, 'The real threat of deepfake pornography: A review of Canadian policy' (2021) 24(3) *Cyberpsychology, Behavior, and Social Networking* 203, 205.

[286] Ibid.

[287] Ibid 203.

[288] Ibid 204.

whether material is a deepfake is complex and difficult. It is particularly challenging as often videos are partially real, but partially tampered with, and as such are 'augmented reality'. Current deepfake detectors find it challenging to spot this nuance – as detectors usually classify videos in binary fashion as entirely real or entirely fake.[289] Detectors also find identifying deepfakes a challenge as deepfake manipulation can be of varying types, such as auditory, visual or both.[290] Studies have been undertaken which show that (unhelpfully) social media platforms can make it *more difficult* to detect deepfakes – so if one is *defamed by an AI tool* in the form of a deepfake and then it spreads online through social media (leading to a crossover with the *defamation by social media* scenario) it can be even more challenging to find redress. Gambín et al. explain: 'some manipulations are performed by social media networks before uploading any content. This is known as social media laundering and removes clues with respect to underlying forgeries, and eventually increases false positive detection rates.'[291]

Blockchain technology shows promise in terms of developing more accurate deepfake detection mechanisms in future.[292] Requiring 'proof of authenticity', or proof of source, can establish which videos are real or deepfakes, and blockchain allows the transfer of information to be highly controlled and verified at each stage, through 'transactional transparency'.[293] So-called smart contracts can also be used to determine who handles a video at any given time, to help ascertain if a video is real – and if not, who has altered the video to create a deepfake, so that they may individually be actioned against in defamation law or otherwise. To more comprehensively

---

[289] Gambín et al. (n 284) 12.
[290] Ibid.
[291] Ibid 13.
[292] Ibid.
[293] Ibid 16.

tackle the spread of deepfakes online, social media sites must be proactive and champion testing new ways to combat the rapid spread of disinformation on their platforms.[294] If social media sites robustly safeguard against the spread of deepfakes this may reduce the need for defamation law as an imperfect medium through which claimants may seek recourse. A broad mobilized response to deepfake production is necessary in order to tackle their wide spread – corporations, the media and governments must work together to recognize their threat to personality interests, human rights and human dignity.[295]

A further question is what area of law is best suited to tackle the emergence of deepfakes. As argued, defamation using deepfake technology is yet another form of *defamation by an AI tool* and English defamation law is a possible recourse through which claimants may attempt to seek redress. However, this is far from an ideal solution, as the requirements to make out an action in defamation (a defamatory statement, the serious harm threshold, reference to the claimant, publication) are many and varied and subject to a broad array of defences. There is also as yet little case law in this area, so it is unclear how sympathetic the common law will in fact be to such a claim, despite the powerful arguments in favour of liability rehearsed earlier in this chapter. Given that the harm caused by pornographic deepfakes is so severe, it is more appropriate that criminal law regulates this area. The UK's recent Online Safety Act 2023 criminalizes the sharing of 'intimate' deepfake images.[296] The police encourage people to report intimate deepfakes, so that those sharing these

---

[294] Ibid.

[295] Ibid.

[296] Section 188 Online Safety Act 2023, amending s 66B Sexual Offences Act 2003. For further reading see 'Criminalising deepfakes: The UK's new offences following the Online Safety Act' (*Herbert Smith* Freehills, 21 May 2024) www.herbertsmithfreehills.com/notes/tmt/2024-05/criminalising-deepfakes-the-uks-new-offences-following-the-online-safety-act accessed 20 December 2024.

images can face prosecution.[297] Further criminal legislation on this issue is expected, with some additional forthcoming legislation 'washed up' in the wake of the November 2024 UK general election.[298] The recent Data (Use and Access) Act 2025 includes further provisions to combat deepfakes in clause 138, providing that it is an offence to create,[299] or intentionally request the creation of, a 'purported intimate image of another person (B)' without B's consent. This amends the Sexual Offences Act 2003.[300] It is argued here that regardless of the fact that *defamation by an AI tool* should be actionable under English defamation law, it is important that the very serious harm rendered by pornographic deepfakes is dealt with through the medium of criminal prosecution, befitting the severity it deserves as a sex offence. There seems to be a strong appetite among the public in many countries to deal with this issue using criminal law means.[301] That is not to say that defamation law does not have a place in regulating deepfakes; it may be more appropriate for an action regarding a deepfake that is reputationally damaging but not pornographic. For the reasons outlined in section 'c. Who should be responsible for an AI tool's defamatory speech?', AI program manufacturers who produce

---

[297] 'Deepfakes: Reporting it to us' (*Police.uk*) www.police.uk/advice/advice-and-information/deepfakes/deepfakes/deepfakes-report-it/#:~:text=It's%20illegal%20to%20share%20or,report%20this%20to%20the%20police accessed 20 December 2024.

[298] That went towards criminalizing the creation of such images. See Ministry of Justice and Laura Farris, 'Government cracks down on "deepfakes" creation' (*GOV.UK*, 16 April 2024) www.gov.uk/government/news/government-cracks-down-on-deepfakes-creation accessed 20 December 2024.

[299] See Data (Use and Access) Act 2025 clause 138. This amends the Sexual Offences Act 2003 accordingly. See https://www.legislation.gov.uk/ukpga/2025/18/enacted accessed 23 July 2025.

[300] Ibid

[301] Matthew B. Kugler and Carly Pace, 'Deepfake privacy: Attitudes and regulation' (2021) 116 *Northwestern University Law Review*, 611, 611.

tools with which to create deepfakes should be potentially liable in defamation law, as well as publishers of the content. In relation to this type of technology, the argument that a manufacturing company had 'done enough' to ensure accuracy of output data of an AI tool falls away when a program is specifically designed to create deepfakes – as defamation is overtly likely, rather than an unintended consequence. Many tools that optimize the creation of deepfakes are already in existence. As Karasavva and Noorbhai observe: 'Scraper or DownAlbum allow users to download all pictures and videos uploaded on publicly available Instagram and Facebook accounts. Thus, using these tools one can easily create the datasets necessary to train the deepfake algorithm'.[302]

It may also be possible to use the aged tort of *Wilkinson v Downton*,[303] which affords liability for the intentional infliction of emotional harm as an alternative route to redress in tortious deepfake cases. However, more recent decisions on the *Wilkinson* rule, such as *Wainwright* and *Rhodes*,[304] have set claimants a high bar of a conduct, mental and consequence element to be overcome.[305] In any event, it is outside the scope of this work to discuss this further.

III. Concluding remarks for Part II

This part of this chapter has considered two technological eventualities of online defamation: third-party comments containing defamatory material in the *third-party poster* scenario and *defamation by AI tool*, be it by a generative LLM hallucinating or the more malevolent method of a reputationally damaging deepfake. Both of these are new scenarios that have been

---

[302] Karasavva and Noorbhai (n 285) 204.
[303] Ibid 206 and *Wilkinson v Downton* [1897] EWHC 1 (QB).
[304] *Wainwright v Home Office* [2003] UKHL 53 [46]–[47].
[305] *Rhodes v OPO and Another* [2015] UKSC 32 [73]–[87].

brought to the fore by technological advancements of the digital revolution since the early 2000s, and both scenarios pose unique legal challenges for the traditional area of English defamation law. The prevalence of defamation by AI and the sheer number of third-party comments on social media (and other) websites has increased the defamatory potential of the internet exponentially. It has been argued that the s 5 defence in the 2013 Act provides a powerful incentive for web hosts to act in accordance with the relevant statutory instrument, providing a fair balance between the interests of those defamed online seeking redress and web hosts themselves, as well as free expression online. The approach of the 2013 Act in this regard must be commended, although there are still outstanding issues posed by s 5 (such as whether social media websites are caught in its remit and the fact that no interim relief pending trial is available for potentially defamatory third-party posts). Further, it has been argued here that there is no clear reason why reputational damage through an *AI tool* should not be taken seriously under English defamation law. In order to ensure redress, AI tool manufacturers must be held legally responsible in English defamation law for creating an AI program that defames, subject to requisite demonstration of rigorous accuracy checking on the part of manufacturers during product development. Finally, deepfakes are a deeply concerning phenomena that pose some of the most potentially grievous potential to reputation, personal dignity, self-perception and human rights. While defamation law is an avenue that could be pursued to combat these creations ex post, thankfully English criminal law has begun to criminalize sharing the most harmful types of deepfakes, those of a sexual nature.

★★★

Conclusion for Chapter 3

Chapter 3 as a whole has argued that a number of different changes have made it uniquely difficult for claimants who are the victims of online defamation to bring a successful action in England and Wales. Firstly, the law was partially reformed by the Defamation Act 2013, just over a decade ago at the worst possible time. Online defamation was beginning to gain pace, yet the 2013 Act's sympathies primarily lie with defendants and the Act openly prioritizes freedom of expression at the expense of reputation. Part I focused on the introduction of ss 1 and 8 Defamation Act 2013 as two examples of changes the law brought in that particularly disadvantage claimants in online defamation cases. Secondly, in Part II, this chapter considered the defence for 'host' websites in s 5 of the Defamation Act 2013 as a (lone) example of good practice introduced by the Defamation Act 2013 and placed it in the context of Strasbourg jurisprudence. Finally, it was argued here that defamation law can and should do more to protect claimants defamed by AI tool, a scenario rendered increasingly likely due to the burgeoning widespread use of generative LLMs.

FOUR

Routes to Remedy? The 'Right to Be Forgotten' as an Alternative Route to Redress

Introduction

Chapter 3 of this book has argued that, for a number of different reasons, English defamation law is currently unsatisfactory in protecting the reputation – and therefore personal dignity – of those defamed online, in light of the prevailing threat of defamation by *social media*, *AI tools* and *third-party posters* in the digital age. Defamation law is largely insufficient in this goal for two main reasons: firstly, the substance of the action in English defamation law is now increasingly difficult to make out, partly due to changes introduced by the Defamation Act 2013. Secondly, defamation law is not doing enough to tackle phenomena produced by technological advancements (such as defamation by *AI* and *third-party posters*). An increasingly liberal interpretation of the law in favour of claimants must be adopted in such scenarios if meaningful redress is to be achieved.

In particular, the serious harm threshold in s 1(1) of the Defamation Act 2013 can act as a significant obstacle to those defamed on the internet, as it raises the bar from the previous common law position, meaning that more claims will be struck out at this stage. As explained in Chapter 3, Part I, the judiciary's interpretation of s 1 as biased in favour of 'evidentiary' arguments means that it may be more challenging to meet this threshold if an individual is a victim of defamation online, rather than by traditional mediums. The single publication rule in s 8 Defamation Act 2013 that limits defendant liability disadvantages all potential claimants, but particularly those who have been defamed on the web – as the internet has the unbridled potential to bring information from the distant past to the surface at any time. Defamation law is also ill-equipped to meet some of the technological issues raised by online defamation. It has been argued in the previous chapter that *defamation by AI tool* is a very real threat, looming heavily on the horizon given the incumbent Prime Minister's recent promise to integrate AI into daily lives.[1] If this fails to be taken seriously by the courts, then this will lead to a growing lacuna in the protection of reputation online. It has also been argued that the s 5 defence for operators of websites should be interpreted to include conglomerates such as Facebook and X in the *defamation by social media* scenario, to incentivize large social media websites to act in accordance with the annexed statutory regulations. However, it remains to be seen if the law is interpreted in the ways suggested by Chapter 3, particularly now that defamation law has 'swung' in favour of freedom of expression.[2] It is far from certain this will, in fact, happen.

Given the rather bleak picture painted for obtaining redress in such matters in defamation law, this book now turns to an alternate method of redress: UK data protection law, inherited from the EU. The *right to be forgotten* (RTBF), is a broad erasure mechanism that allows 'data subjects' to obtain the removal of their personal data on the internet, enshrined in Article 17 of the General Data Protection Regulation (GDPR).[3] The

---

[1] See 'Prime Minister sets out blueprint to turbocharge AI' (*GOV.UK*, 12 January 2025) www.gov.uk/government/news/prime-minister-sets-out-blueprint-to-turbocharge-ai accessed 23 January 2025.

[2] Alastair Mullis and Andrew Scott, 'The swing of the pendulum: Reputation, expression and the recentering of English libel law' (2012) 61(3) *Northern Ireland Legal Quarterly* 27.

[3] Regulation (EU) 2016/679 of the European Parliament and of the Council on the protection of natural persons with regard to the processing

GDPR lives on after Brexit in the UK jurisdiction as inherited (now domestic) law, termed the 'UK GDPR'. As has been recognized in an embryonic way by the English courts, both data protection law and defamation law work a twin purpose to protect different aspects of a claimant's private life and it is logical to consider both causes of action in tandem in cases of online libel.[4]

★★★

Part I: What is the right to be forgotten?

I. Background context

The GDPR is a revolutionary piece of law making, designed to champion data protection rights for individuals across Europe by setting a high standard in the form of an overarching regulation, transplanted directly into member state legislatures. European commissioners involved in drafting the GDPR commented that a goal of the EU in enacting the GDPR was for this to become a 'standard setter' for the protection of

---

of personal data and on the free movement of such data, and repealing Directive 95/46/EC (GDPR) [2016] OJ L119/1 (27/4/2016).

[4] As was held in *Prince Moulay v Elaph Publishing* [2017] EWCA Civ 29. See Simon Brown, 'Case law: *Prince Moulay v Elaph Publishing*, Moroccan prince wins libel and data protection appeal against Arabic news publisher' (*Inforrm*, 7 February 2017) https://inforrm.org/2017/02/07/case-law-prince-moulay-v-elaph-publishing-moroccan-prince-wins-libel-and-data-protection-appeal-against-arabic-news-publisher-simon-brown/ accessed 25 May 2025. See also *Pacini & Anor v Dow Jones & Co Inc* [2024] EWHC 1709 (KB), where HHJ Parkes KC refused to strike out a defamation claim 'disguised' as a data protection claim [55] as per Jeevan Hariharan, 'Case comment: *Pacini v Dow Jones*, a call for appellate intervention on reputational harm damages' (*Inforrm*, 11 July 2024) https://inforrm.org/2024/07/11/case-comment-pacini-v-dow-jones-a-call-for-appellate-intervention-on-reputational-harm-damages-jeevan-hariharan/ accessed 25 May 2025.

personality interests in the digital age.[5] Aside from the desire to galvanize global change in robustly defending personal data, the drafting of the GDPR was also reactionary. It succeeded the previous data protection framework at EU level – the Data Protection Directive 1995 – which was increasingly seen as out of date due to the vast technological advancements between 1995 and 2012, the latter year being the time of the GDPR's first public release in draft form.[6] Two years after the EU Commission released its first lengthy draft of the GDPR, a seminal case was handed down by the Court of Justice of the European Union (CJEU): *Google Spain*.[7] The timing of the surprising ruling in *Google Spain* was most interesting,[8] as it came at a point when the RTBF, as included in the draft GDPR, was garnering hostility from legal commentators.[9] This was despite the fact the RTBF was far from an entirely new concept: France had already implemented a *droit à l'oubli* (a right to erasure) in its domestic law.[10] The right to private and family life and the right to control one's personal data are

---

[5] Viviane Reding, 'The EU Data Protection Reform 2012: Making Europe the standard setter for modern data protection rules in the digital age' (22 January 2012) http://europa.eu/rapid/press-release_SPEECH-12-26_en.htm accessed 18 June 2015.

[6] Directive 95/46/EC of the European Parliament and of the Council of 24 October 1995 on the protection of individuals with regard to the processing of personal data and of the free movement of such data [1995] OJ L 281, 31.

[7] Case C-131/12 *Google Spain SL and Another v Agencia Española de protección de Datos (AEPD) and Another* [2014] WLR 659, ECLI:EU:C:2014:317.

[8] Daniel Solove, 'What Google must forget: The EU ruling on the right to be forgotten' (*LinkedIn*, 13 May 2014) www.linkedin.com/pulse/20140513230300-2259773-what-google-must-forget-the-eu-ruling-on-the-right-to-be-forgotten accessed 23 January 2025.

[9] See, for example, Meg L Ambrose and Jef Ausloos, 'The right to be forgotten across the pond' (2013) 3 *Journal of Information Law and Policy* 1.

[10] Ibid 1.

also both codified in Articles 7 and 8 of the EU Charter of Fundamental Rights.[11]

One of the reasons that the RTBF enshrined in the draft GDPR 2012 had generated worldwide publicity was because European citizens did not believe the regulation's predecessor, the Data Protection Directive 1995, contained a right of erasure.[12] Indeed, a key motivating factor for the inception of the proposed regulation was to strengthen current insufficient data privacy rights and enhance a data subject's control over private information.[13] It was therefore surprising when the CJEU declared in *Google Spain* that a limited right to deletion already existed in EU law and could be found within Articles 6, 12 and 14 of the Data Protection Directive 1995.[14] Although the right within *Google Spain* manifested itself as a delisting of a search result on Google, the delisting right expounded in the judgment had the potential to be used in future cases to delete substantive personal data directly from websites. It is not an exaggeration to suggest that this judgment sent a shockwave through the worldwide legal community. Academics immediately responded to the judgment, a considerable amount of press coverage was generated and Google began to take measures to implement the ruling.[15]

Despite the significant publicity garnered, it is important to note that the CJEU *did not* create a generalized RTBF in the judgment of *Google Spain* in the same way that one exists to

---

[11] Charter of Fundamental Rights of the European Union (18/2/2000) OJ C 364/3, Article 7 and Article 8 www.europarl.europa.eu/charter/pdf/text_en.pdf accessed 23 January 2025.
[12] See (n 1).
[13] See Reding (n 5).
[14] See *Google Spain* (n 7) and Directive 95/46/EC (n 6).
[15] Paul Bernal, 'Are Google intentionally overreacting to the right to be forgotten?' (*Inforrm Blog*, 4 July 2014) https://inforrm.wordpress.com/2014/07/04/are-google-intentionally-overreacting-to-the-right-to-be-forgotten-paul-bernal/ accessed 30 January 2025.

this day in Article 17 GDPR. For the purposes of this book a RTBF is defined as a comprehensive personal data removal right, such as that enshrined within Article 17 GDPR (and UK GDPR). Rather, the CJEU construed a limited *deletion* right was present within the Data Protection 1995 (DPD '95). This deletion right was lifted from a combination of Articles 12 and 14 of the Directive. Article 12 of the DPD '95 predominantly relates to data removal in situations where data is outdated or inaccurate and Article 14 of the DPD '95 includes a 'right to object' to data processing on 'justified' grounds.[16] Despite its broad interpretation of the existing law, *Google Spain* did not create a generalized RTBF; in order to invoke *Google Spain*'s deletion right, a data subject must prove that the information is no longer relevant or that the data is inaccurate or excessive. In *Google Spain*, the CJEU adjudicated on three questions. Firstly, it was asked to decide whether a deletion right could be invoked within current EU data protection law.[17] Secondly, the court gave judgment upon whether the DPD '95 applied to Google as its company base was in the US (and not the EU).[18] Lastly, it ruled upon whether Google as a search engine could be construed as a 'data controller' for the purposes of the DPD '95.[19] Unexpectedly, the CJEU answered all three questions affirmatively.

Momentum grew after this shock ruling and the newly renamed 'right to erasure' (still a comprehensive RTBF) remained intact in Article 17 of the GDPR despite its passage through the EU legislative process, becoming enforceable in all member states – including the UK – in 2018. The 'right to erasure' in Article 17 is still widely referred to by its initial name in early GDPR drafts – the *right to be forgotten* – and as both names still accurately reflect the right, both will be used interchangeably in this book to refer to Article 17.

---

[16] Directive 95/46/EC (n 6) Article 14 'The data subject's right to object'.
[17] *Google Spain* (n 7) [92]–[93].
[18] Ibid [60].
[19] Ibid [38].

II. Article 17 GDPR

Article 17 allows 'data subjects' (identifiable individuals to whom information online relates)[20] to obtain from 'data controllers' (including website hosts, authors of a webpage or post and search engines)[21] deletion of personal data concerning themselves online. It also contains a requirement for controllers to contact third parties in relation to the replication or repetition of personal data that has been requested for deletion under Article 17(2). The right is broadly framed, with the mentioned roles loosely defined,[22] and does not require a threshold of seriousness to be met to invoke the right.[23] Article 17 appears to apply both to information initially uploaded to the internet by a data subject themselves and personal information uploaded by a third party. A limitation on the right is in the form of Article 17(3)(a), which contains an exception relating to the exercise of freedom of expression of the data controller,[24] as well as the GDPR's journalism exemption in the form of 'special purposes'.[25] Article 17 states:

1. The data subject shall have the right to *obtain from the controller the erasure of personal data* concerning him or her without undue delay and the controller shall have the obligation to erase personal data without undue delay where one of the following grounds applies:

---

[20] UK GDPR, Article 4(1).

[21] See *Google Spain* (n 7), where the CJEU found that search engine Google could constitute a data controller, and see UK GDPR, Article 4(7).

[22] UK GDPR, Article 4.

[23] As opposed to a defamation claim brought under the Defamation Act 2013, s 1.

[24] UK GDPR, Article 17(3)(a).

[25] EU GDPR, Article 85.

(a) the personal data are *no longer necessary* in relation to the purposes for which they were collected or otherwise processed;

(b) the data subject *withdraws consent* on which the processing is based according to point (a) of Article 6(1), or point (a) of Article 9(2), and where there is no other legal ground for the processing;

(c) the data subject objects to the processing pursuant to Article 21(1) and there are no overriding legitimate grounds for the processing, or the data subject objects to the processing pursuant to Article 21(2);

(d) the personal data have been unlawfully processed;

(e) the personal data have to be erased for compliance with a legal obligation under domestic law;

(f) the personal data have been collected in relation to the offer of information society services referred to in Article 8(1);

[(g) the personal data have been processed as a result of an allegation about the data subject –
  (i) which was made by a person who is a malicious person in relation to the data subject (whether they became such a person before or after the allegation was made),
  (ii) which has been investigated by the controller, and
  (iii) in relation to which the controller has decided that no further action is to be taken.]

2. Where the controller has made the personal data public and is obliged pursuant to paragraph 1 to erase the personal data, the controller, taking account of available technology and the cost of implementation, shall take reasonable steps, including technical measures, to inform controllers which are processing the personal data that the data subject has requested the erasure by such controllers of any links to, or copy or replication of, those personal data.

3. Paragraphs 1 and 2 shall not apply to the extent that processing is necessary:
   (a) for exercising *the right of freedom of expression* and information.[26]

In relation to Article 17(1)(b), an erasure right could become engaged in a scenario where consent to processing has initially been given by data subject and subsequently revoked, with no time limit in operation.[27] In the case of an online publication of potentially defamatory personal information, an individual could argue that they revoke any previous consent they may have given to that information being processed (for example, the prior use of a social media website in the *defamation by social media* scenario). In the event they gave no prior consent to its processing, an individual could claim that the false and defamatory personal data has otherwise been unlawfully processed, which would be particularly relevant if the false and defamatory personal data was uploaded to the internet by a third party, in according to Article 17(1)(d), in the *third-party poster* scenario. A person defamed online could also require erasure of the personal data on the grounds of objecting to the information's processing according to Article 17(1)(c).[28] The UK GDPR has extraterritorial effect, as it applies to

---

[26] UK GDPR; emphasis added. Note Article 17(1)(g) was added by the Victims and Prisoners Act 2024, s 31. This addition therefore does not appear in the EU GDPR or Article 17 as originally enacted. A further paragraph was also added to Article 17 UK GDPR by s 31, that details a 'malicious person' is one who has been convicted of one of a number of offences as set out by s 31(5) against a given victim, including harassment and stalking. See s 31(3) of the Act for more details. The impact of this section is to therefore expand Article 17 and to further protect victims of harassment and stalking. This expansion is to be welcomed, although it is not a central concern of this book.

[27] As this would, it is submitted here, come under the remit of Article 17(1)(a).

[28] This works in conjunction with Article 21 UK GDPR, the 'right to object'.

those 'offering goods or services to individuals in the UK';[29] such a service could be offered by, for example, a social media website which may be domiciled outside of the UK. As such, it is an extremely powerful erasure right, with a large scope – exactly what is necessary for tackling the multi-jurisdictional issue of online invasions of privacy – and in the case of this book – reputation.

There are, of course, a number of exemptions to Article 17's erasure right. Article 17 goes on to explain: 'Paragraphs 1 and 2 shall not apply to the extent that processing is necessary: (a) for exercising the right of freedom of expression and information.'[30]

In terms of this book, the most pertinent exemption is Article 17(3)(a).[31] In this sense, there is a distinct similarity between defamation law and data protection law here: both the RTBF and a claim in defamation will chiefly be balanced against competing arguments that the publication (and continued access) of the personal information is in the public interest. How this balancing exercise should be conducted in relation to the RTBF will be returned to a later point in this chapter.

Finally, it is important to observe that a data controller's compliance with an Article 17 erasure request has a large motivating factor – the considerable sanctions possible under the UK GDPR (for non-compliance). Article 17 entails a fine of either £17,500,000 or 4 per cent of turnover according Article 83(5)(a) and (b).[32] The UK GDPR also notes that the decision to impose either the fine or the turnover tariff will depend on *whichever is higher*.[33] This is a considerable amount of money even for a large data controller such as Facebook or

---

[29] See the Information Commissioner's Office, 'The UK GDPR' https://ico.org.uk/for-organisations/data-protection-and-the-eu/data-protection-and-the-eu-in-detail/the-uk-gdpr/ accessed 30 January 2025. Also see UK GDPR, Article 3(1) and (2)(a).
[30] UK GDPR, Article 17(3); emphasis added.
[31] Also see EU GDPR, Article 85(1).
[32] UK GDPR.
[33] UK GDPR, Article 83(5).

Google and an inordinately large sum for a smaller corporation. Indeed, in Article 83's opening paragraph, the UK GDPR notes that one of the aims of the fines is to be 'dissuasive'.[34]

Now the groundwork has been set, this chapter will turn to a substantive comparison between the RTBF as a route to redress for those defamed online, in comparison to traditional English defamation law.

★★★

Part II: Can the 'right to be forgotten' provide a more effective remedy than English defamation law?

The comparison conducted here between English defamation law and the RTBF will be navigated by individual points pertinent to those seeking redress against false and potentially defamatory material on the internet.

I. Accessibility of redress

Despite the complex terminology that data protection law is couched in, the RTBF is a straightforward remedy. Ultimately, all an individual must do to assert their Article 17 erasure right is to contract a data controller and request the information's removal from the internet. In the case of the *defamation by social media* scenario, it is straightforward to ascertain who a potential controller is – either the website themselves or, alternatively, the person who has posted the offending statement in question. This is because Article 4(7) UK GDPR has a wide definition of 'data controller' as either an entity or a natural person that determines the processing of personal data – and processing, according to Article 4(2), catches almost all functions one could perform with information, such as 'structuring,

---

[34] UK GDPR, Article 83(1).

storage, adaptation or alteration, retrieval, consultation, use, disclosure by transmission, dissemination or otherwise making available'.[35] Similarly, if a person is defamed by an *AI tool* such as a chatbot on a AI website, one could contact the website as a controller for those purposes, or any third party who further disseminates the information online. This route to remedy is clearly not as lengthy, costly or complex as mounting a formal legal action in defamation. On instruction of a law firm to argue a case in defamation, the wait to trial in the English and Welsh jurisdiction would also likely be significant,[36] as both County Court and High Court waiting times in the wake of the COVID-19 pandemic are lengthy,[37] and prove a very real barrier to the sort of swift justice one would wish to obtain in defamation – as the longer the defamatory remark is able to percolate online, the more harm to reputation (and personal dignity) accrues. Conversely, to invoke the RTBF, all, in theory, an individual needs to do is to request the information's erasure from a data controller. This initial point of contact would be quick to make – those defamed online could likely make contact with a controller by email. There will, of course, be a waiting time between this request and any response, although large conglomerates such as Google now appear to have streamlined processes for such a request down to a fine art, with particular forms that need to be filled out by the data subject,[38] and specific teams responsible and

---

[35] UK GDPR, Article 4(2).

[36] See John Hyde, 'Litigants now wait 78 weeks for their County Court date' (*Civil Mediation Council*, 2023) https://civilmediation.org/78-weeks-wait-for-court-date/ accessed 24 January 2025.

[37] See ACSO, 'Record court waiting times mean UK has a third-rate justice system' (7 December 2023) https://acso.org.uk/news/202312/record-court-waiting-times-mean-uk-has-third-rate-justice-system accessed 24 January 2025.

[38] See Google, 'Legal help: Right to be forgotten overview' https://support.google.com/legal/answer/10769224?hl=en-GB accessed 24 January 2025.

dedicated to handling the requests.[39] Of course, if the data controller refuses to comply and the individual concerned is not satisfied with any explanation given for refusing the request (such as linked to a relevant exemption), the matter could then be referred to the UK's Information Commissioner's Office and ultimately be adjudicated in court – which would mean that the litigant would suffer the same lengthy wait times as they would pursuing an action in traditional defamation law. However, there is every chance that this will not happen – many erasure requests are straightforwardly upheld after a request is lodged, and it has been reported that Google has deleted approximately 2.5 million web links since 2014.[40] This option for a timely remedy of personal data erased (be it false and defamatory or otherwise) is something that defamation law, unlike the RBTF, simply cannot provide.

Further, the cost of litigation is another area where the RTBF will likely have an advantage for those seeking redress when defamed online, in comparison to an action in defamation law. The 'Wagatha Christie' defamation litigation in 2021 demonstrated the sheer cost of launching (and defending) a libel trial, 'with costs for both parties estimated to be in excess of 1 million'.[41] In the event that a defamation case is lost by a claimant – which, as demonstrated by the previous chapter, is always possible due to the many different hurdles a defamation claim can fall at – then a *defendant's* costs are

---

[39] Cohen Davis Solicitors, 'Right to be forgotten' https://arighttobeforgotten.co.uk/right-to-be-forgotten-google#:~:text=Between%20June%202014%20and%20November,to%20nearly%204%20million%20links last accessed 24 January 2025.

[40] See 'How many people in Europe use their "right to be forgotten" online?' (*Surfshark*, 28 February 2024) https://surfshark.com/blog/right-to-be-forgotten-requests accessed 24 January 2025.

[41] James Martin, 'High profile case shines light on expensive costs in defamation claims' (*Blacks Solicitors*, 16 May 2022) www.lawblacks.com/2022/05/16/high-profile-case-shines-light-on-expensive-costs-in-defamation-claims/ accessed 24 January 2025.

likely to be absorbed by the claimant as well as their own, as was the case for Rebekah Vardy in *Vardy v Rooney*. Ms Vardy was recently ordered to pay 90 per cent of defendant Coleen Rooney's legal costs on top of her own legal fees, Rooney's costs amounting to £1.8 million pounds[42] (an order she sought to challenge, although the matter is now settled).[43] This serves to show that lengthy costs disputes in defamation can also prolong defamation litigation and, somewhat ironically, generate even higher legal bills for an unsuccessful claimant. The peril of an ordinary individual seeking to fund an action in defamation, much less pay an opposing party's costs, is a powerful disincentive for individuals seeking to use defamation law to obtain a remedy. This is in contrast with the RTBF, where an initial erasure request can simply be made to a data controller – by either email, form or letter – free of charge. If the matter does not escalate to litigation, then no costs will be accrued. Contacting the UK's Information Commissioner's Officer (ICO) to obtain information is also free of charge, with the ICO potentially acting as an intervener if the matter were to be escalated to a court.[44]

Finally, the RTBF has the advantage of simplicity over any potential litigation in defamation law. The public are readily

---

[42] *Vardy v Rooney* [2021] EWHC 1888 (QB) and Julie Hamilton, '"How much?" Wagatha Christie trial back in the headlines' (*Morton Fraser Macroberts*, 8 October 2024) www.mfmac.com/insights/litigation-disp ute-resolution/how-much-wagatha-christie-trial-back-in-the-headlines/#:~:text=The%20news%20of%20the%20%22sheer,have%20reached%20%C2%A31.8M accessed 24 January 2025.

[43] Adele Whaley and Kirstie Goulder, '*Vardy v Rooney*: The saga continues (the costs era)' (*Greenwoods*, 29 October 2024) www.greenwoods.co.uk/article/vardy-v-rooney-the-saga-continues-the-costs-era/ accessed 24 January 2025 and see Paul Glynn, 'Vardy must pay £1.4m of Rooney's "Wagatha" legal costs' *(BBC News*, 6 May 2025) https://www.bbc.co.uk/news/articles/c7939wwxd0jo accessed 23 July 2025.

[44] As was the case in *NT1 and NT2 v Google LLC (Intervenor: The Information Commissioner)* [2018] EWHC 799 (QB).

aware of their RTBF: as discussed earlier in this chapter, the *Google Spain* judgment handed down by the CJEU in 2014 achieved widespread academic, political and press attention across Europe, as well as Article 17's presence in early drafts of the EU Commission's 2012 GDPR.[45] Therefore, people may be feel increasingly confident to write to data controllers and request the removal of information, with the awareness that such a right not only exists, but is now commonplace. There is evidence that people are utilizing the RTBF in large numbers: between 2014 and 2020, nearly 4 million links were requested for deletion by Google.[46] Writing to a data controller, or filling in a relevant form to request a RTBF, is typically also far more straightforward than engaging a solicitor (who then instructs a barrister) and mounting a trial in defamation, and it is considerably less daunting to those not familiar with the legal system.

II. Hurdles to making a claim

One of the strongest arguments in favour of the RTBF as a method of obtaining redress for those defamed online (in comparison to defamation law) is the lack of legal hurdles

---

[45] See, for example, European Union Committee, 'EU Data Protection Law: A "Right to be forgotten"?' (HL 2nd report of session 2014–15) paper 40; Meg L Ambrose, 'It's about time: Privacy, information life cycles, and the right to be forgotten' (2013) 16(2) *Stanford Technology Law Review* 369; Jeffrey Rosen, 'The right to be forgotten' (2012) *Stanford Law Review Online* 88; Diane L Zimmerman, 'The "new" privacy and the "old": Is applying the tort law of privacy like putting high button shoes on the internet?' (2012) 17 *Communications Law and Policy* 107; Paul Schwartz, 'The EU–US privacy collision: A turn to institutions and procedures' (2013) 126 *Harvard Law Review* 1966; and W. Gregory Voss, 'One year and loads of data later, where are we? An update on the proposed European Union General Data Protection Regulation' (2013) 16(10) *Journal of Internet Law* 13.

[46] See (n 39).

necessary to be surmounted to assert the right. If a person withdraws consent to processing, objects to said personal data's processing or the processing is otherwise unlawful or unnecessary,[47] as discussed in earlier in this chapter, an individual can invoke their Article 17 rights. The definition of 'personal data' in the UK GDPR is similarly extremely broad:

> 'personal data' means any information relating to an identified or identifiable natural person ('data subject'); an identifiable natural person is one who can be identified, directly or indirectly, in particular by reference to an identifier such as a name, an identification number, location data, an online identifier or to one or more factors specific to the physical, physiological, genetic, mental, economic, cultural or social identity of that natural person.[48]

This catches all (potentially) defamatory statements made online that reference the given claimant. The very point of the RTBF is that it is one of a number of data subject rights introduced by the GDPR to rebalance the control over personal information online against unbridled free expression.[49] The central thesis behind the GDPR's adoption was that more needed to be done to protect personal data online,[50] and by very essence, reliance on the right was intended to be easy and the right strong. The only requirement to initially invoke the right is that the information in question must be personal data, which, as can be seen earlier in this chapter, is broadly defined. As shown through the analysis conducted in Chapter 3, a plethora of legal hurdles must

---

[47] According to UK GDPR, Article 17(1)(a), (b), (c) and (d).
[48] UK GDPR, Article 4(1).
[49] UK GDPR, Articles 12–23.
[50] Reding (n 5).

be met by a claimant for an action in defamation – there must be a defamatory statement, it must meet the serious harm threshold, there must be reference to the claimant and requisite communication (publication). Unlike s 1(1) of the Defamation Act 2013 there is no threshold of severity to invoke the RTBF as it is a broad data right and there is no time constraint operational as to *when* a data subject must invoke their right (such as the limitation period in s 8 Defamation Act 2013), relevant to the *repetition of statements online over a year later* scenario. To the contrary, the Strasbourg Court and the CJEU have both noted that the longer the passage of time between the information in question and the right being invoked, the stronger a claim for the information's removal in the event that a RTBF is contested.[51]

Another barrier that defamation law presents is the number of defences available to defendants on receipt of a defamation lawsuit. Aside from the new s 5 defence that shields operators of host websites,[52] there are numerous other defences operable to defend against a claim, such as the truth defence, honest opinion, publication on a matter of public interest and the (second) new defence introduced by the 2013 Act – protection for those writing in peer-reviewed journals.[53] When reading a judgment in English libel law, it is perhaps the only tort where judicial consideration of defences is often more lengthy than the claim itself. For example, in the High Court decision of *Banks v Cadwalladr* (concerning comments made in a TED talk and a tweet), Mrs Justice Steyn's consideration of a defence amounts to over 300 paragraphs.[54] To compound this, the 2013 reform put the defences of justification, fair comment

---

[51] As was the case in *Google Spain* and *Hurbain v Belgium* (App no 57292/16, 4 July 2023) [220]–[221].
[52] Defamation Act 2013. Discussed at length in Chapter 3.
[53] Section 6 Defamation Act 2013.
[54] *Banks v Cadwalladr* [2022] EWHC 1417 (QB) [100]–[415].

and *Reynolds* on a statutory footing.[55] The rapid pivot of the reform to prioritize expression has meant that aspects of the traditional defences have also been reinterpreted and their scope broadened. As discussed in Chapter 3, honest opinion in s 3 of the Act no longer has to relate to a matter of public interest, which was previously a requirement of the defence at common law.[56] What was previously known as the *Reynolds* defence now lives on in s 4 of the 2013 Act and has undergone the most significant changes from its common law predecessor. Section 4 is quite considerably broader in nature, as the standard of responsible journalism has (at least in statute) been abandoned as a benchmark to rely on the defence: instead, one must have reasonable belief that publication is in the public interest according to s 4(1)(b) and the publication itself must relate to a matter of public interest in s 4(1)(a).[57] This standard is now so wide that so-termed citizen journalists can rely on this defence, in certain circumstances.[58] By way of comparison with the RTBF, the main 'defence' for a data controller to refuse compliance with an erasure request under Article 17 is the 17(3)(a) exception outlined earlier, pertaining to freedom of expression. There is little said about this exemption in the UK (or EU) GDPR itself. If a RTBF request was refused and the matter litigated, to successfully argue that expression should trump an erasure right, the public interest would likely have to be *sufficiently* engaged under Article 17(3)(a). This accords with both Strasbourg and English case law on this matter, particularly in the field of misuse of private

---

[55] Now s 2 (truth), s 3 (honest opinion) and s 4 (publication on a matter of public interest) Defamation Act 2013.

[56] See, for example, *Telnikoff v Matusevitch* [1992] UKHL 2, [1992] 2 AC in 343. Also see Eric Descheemaeker, 'Mapping defamation defences' (2015) 78 *Modern Law Review* 641, 652ff.

[57] Defamation Act 2013.

[58] Such as in *Economou v De Freitas* [2018] EWCA Civ 2591, EMLR 7 and *Hay v Cresswell* [2023] EWHC 882 (KB), EMLR 17.

information – when Article 8 ECHR rights (privacy) and Article 10 (expression) rights must be weighed against each other, in cases such as *Von Hannover* (Nos 1, 2 and 3), *Axel Springer*, *PJS*, *Campbell* and *Ferdinand*.[59] Given that the purpose of the RTBF's drafting was to reinstate the informational autonomy of data subjects, any public interest claim that would negate a RTBF would have to be robustly argued. There are two other relevant 'defences' for the RTBF (for the purposes of this book): the *domestic purposes* exemption and the *journalistic* exemption. The 'domestic purposes' exemption exempts application of the GDPR to 'the processing of personal data by a natural person in the course of a *'purely personal or household activity'*.[60] This, of course, has the potential to include posts to social media. However, case law and academic commentary has shown that if the personal data in question is posted to a large group or audience (as is often the case on social media websites), then the domestic purposes exemption will not apply.[61] In the *defamation by social media* scenario, defamatory posts online will often be public or published to a section of

---

[59] *Von Hannover v Germany*, App no 59320/00 (ECHR, 24 September 2004); *Axel Springer AG v Germany* App no 39954/08 (ECHR, 7 February 2012) App nos 40660/08 and 60641/08 w/ *Von Hannover v Germany (No 2)* (7 February 2012); *Von Hannover v Germany (No 3)* App no 8772/10 (ECHR, 19 September 2013); *PJS (Appellant) v News Group Newspapers Ltd (Respondent)* [2016] UKSC 26; *Campbell v MGN Ltd* [2004] UKHL 22, [2004] 2 AC 457; *Ferdinand v MGN* [2011] EWHC 2454 (QB). More will be said on this balancing exercise and how it should be conducted in RTBF cases later in this chapter.

[60] UK GDPR, Article 2(2)(a).

[61] David Erdos, "Beyond "having a domestic"? Regulatory interpretation of European data protection law and individual publication" (2017) 33(3) *Computer Law and Security Review* 275, 276; and Case C-101/01 *Bodil Lindqvist v Åklagarkammaren i Jönköping* [2003] ECR I-12971 [47]; Fiona Brimblecombe and Gavin Phillipson, 'Regaining digital privacy? The new "right to be forgotten" and online expression' 4(1) *Canadian Journal of Comparative and Contemporary Law* 1, 29.

the public – this is how significant reputational and personal dignity harm is rendered. As such, this exemption should not prove a barrier to invoking a RTBF with respect to potentially defamatory posts on the internet.

There is also a journalism exemption instructed by the GDPR, present in the annexed Data Protection Act (DPA) 2018. In this Act, the journalistic exemption appears in Schedule 2, paragraph 26. It states that if activities are carried out for the 'purposes of journalism'[62] and

> with a view to the publication by a person of journalistic material [and] the controller reasonably believes the publication of the material would be in the public interest … the listed GDPR provisions do not apply to the extent that the controller reasonably believes that the application of those provisions would be incompatible.[63]

These provisions include Article 17. The exemption goes on to issue a caveat: 'in determining whether publication would be in the public interest the controller must take into account the special importance of the public interest in the freedom of expression and information'.[64] This means that a data controller must think it impossible to apply the relevant UK GDPR provision (in this case the RTBF) while acting in a journalistic way.[65] This exemption is reminiscent of Article

---

[62] DPA 2018, Schedule 2, para 26(1).
[63] Ibid para 26, section (2)(a), (b) and section (3).
[64] Ibid para 26, section (4).
[65] See UK Information Commissioner's Office, 'Data protection and journalism: A guide for the media' https://ico.org.uk/media2/for-organisations/documents/1552/data-protection-and-journalism-media-guidance.pdf accessed 14 March 2019; and Hugh Tomlinson, 'The "journalism exemption" in the Data Protection Act: Part I, the law' (*Inforrm*, 28 March 2019) https://inforrm.org/2017/03/28/the-journalism-exemption-in-the-data-protection-act-part-1-the-law-hugh-tomlinson-qc/ accessed 14 March 2019.

17(3)(a) in the sense that it will ultimately collapse into a 'personality interests versus freedom of expression' balancing exercise in the event that a RTBF's refusal is contested on these grounds. It is unclear at this point precisely how broadly the 'public interest' will be construed under Schedule 2, 26(2)(b). As has been demonstrated by misuse of private information case law, the English courts have been known to adopt inconsistent approaches to this concept.[66] Defendants can more persuasively argue that the exemption should apply when the subject matter of the information at issue is of 'great interest to the public'.[67] It is also unclear if citizen journalists will be covered by Schedule 2's journalism exemption. This author has observed elsewhere that the CJEU in *Google Spain* held that search engine Google could *not* rely on the journalism exemption present within the DPD '95,[68] and nor could it in *NT1 and NT2* in the English jurisdiction.[69] Indeed, to allow citizen journalists broad access to the journalistic exemption would carve away the genuine definition of what it is to be a journalist.[70] The 2018 Act suggests that citizen journalists were not intended to be covered by the exemption in most circumstances, as a data controller must adhere to a relevant privacy code.[71] As Mr Justice Warby has stated, not every transmission of ideas on the web is journalistic[72] – and to rely on the journalistic exemption, the publication in question must

---

[66] See *Ferdinand* and *PJS* (n 59).

[67] See, for example, counsel submissions of Bloomberg in *ZXC v Bloomberg* [2017] EWHC 328 (QB) [15].

[68] Brimblecombe and Phillipson (n 61) 34–5.

[69] See *NT1 and NT2* (n 44).

[70] Brimblecombe and Phillipson (n 61) 35–6.

[71] DPA 2018, Schedule 2, Part 5, para 26(5). On codes, see Peter Coe, 'A journalism Standards Code for modern journalism' (2023) 28(2) *Communications Law* 49.

[72] *NT1 and NT2* (n 44) [98]. Also see Peter Coe, *Media Freedom in the Age of Citizen Journalism* (Edward Elgar 2021).

be 'properly characterised as journalism'.[73] As such, it appears that the journalistic defence in the DPA 2018 is now narrower than the s 4 'publication on matter of public interest' defence in the Defamation Act 2013, which relinquished its standard of responsible journalism on codification.[74] It is clear, then, that the broad array of defences operable in the English jurisdiction of defamation law are more numerous and extensive than those present in the UK GDPR.

III. Decision making

Another interesting point of comparison between the RTBF and English defamation law is the body which is responsible for deciding whether a claim is upheld. As explained, in the first instance, a data subject simply writes to a data controller to assert their RTBF and in that sense data controllers make the first – and possibly only – decision about whether information should be erased. This approach comes with advantages and disadvantages. The clear advantages of this process are ease, speed and time. As Google (for example) now receives many such requests, they have a dedicated team in place to assess whether the RTBF applies and whether any exemptions override such a request. Google is most likely to refuse a request not because an exemption applies, but because the request itself does not contain enough information.[75] Google employees involved in the initial assessment exercise also escalate number of requests to a specialist legal team to ensure the most informed decision is made.[76] Factors that may influence a decision to uphold a RTBF include whether a person is in the public eye, the nature of the information and

---

[73] Ibid (*NT1 and NT2*).
[74] Fiona Brimblecombe, 'Section 4 Defamation Act 2013: A tale of two approaches' (2024) 29(3) *Torts Law Journal* 245.
[75] See n 39.
[76] Ibid.

the public interest value of the information.[77] It was clear from the outset that the balancing factors of 'celebrity' and 'nature of the information' on the one hand and 'public interest' on the other would likely be applied to erasure requests by data-controller assessment teams.[78] This is because these are factors that English and Strasbourg courts use when conducting the 'ultimate balancing exercise' between privacy interests and competing freedom of expression concerns.[79] This balancing exercise is also the essence of the Article 17(3)(a) exemption to the RTBF. Other relevant factors to this balance may be: if the person concerned has '*waived*' their right to privacy (or perhaps a good reputation),[80] *circumstances* that the information was obtained in and if the information relates to a *private or public place*.[81] From the little information we know about what goes on in online conglomerates, it appears that at least some of these factors are being utilized to assess whether an erasure request under Article 17 is upheld. However, it is important to note that this range of guiding principles have not always been used logically by the Strasbourg and English courts and there is always the risk that data controllers – being less well versed in legal precedent – may interpret these factors in a way which unfairly negatively impacts a legitimate RTBF request. For example, the European Court of Human Rights (ECtHR) has made it clear that even if someone is a public figure, they

---

[77] Ibid.

[78] Fiona Brimblecombe, 'The public interest in deleted personal data? The right to be forgotten's freedom of expression exceptions examined through the lens of Article 10 ECHR' (2020) 23(10) *Journal of Internet Law* 1.

[79] See, for example, Paul Wragg, 'Protecting private information of public interest: Campbell's great promise, unfulfilled' (2015) 7(2) *Journal of Media Law* 225 and Rebecca Moosavian, 'A just balance or just imbalance? The role of metaphor in misuse of private information' (2015) 7(2) *Journal of Media Law* 196.

[80] Which will be returned to later in the discussion of *Hurbain*.

[81] Brimblecombe and Phillipson (n 61).

still have a 'legitimate expectation of the protection of and respect for his or her private life' under Article 8 European Convention on Human Rights (ECHR).[82] Therefore, any decision automatically refusing a RTBF request on the basis that the person asserting it is well known is a misinterpretation of precedent.[83] There have been academic concerns voiced about the validity of the balancing criteria expounded by the English courts, particularly in relation to factors going to the weight of a competing expression interest.[84] Most notably, the 'role model argument' (which states that if a claimant is a role model that the information in question should lean towards publication) and the 'right to criticise' (which argues that information should be published if it prompts debate) are two of the more egregious examples of poorly reasoned 'balancing factors' employed by the English courts in this respect.[85] These missteps come as a stark warning that any balancing exercise articulated either by data controllers or the judiciary in assessing whether the RTBF is upheld must be trod carefully if similar mistakes are to be avoided. The RTBF presents an opportunity to articulate a new set of balancing factors more appropriate for the digital age; this course has begun to be chartered – with mixed success – via the 2023 case of *Hurbain* at the Grand Chamber of the ECtHR.[86] In the case, the Grand Chamber applied a modified version of previously articulated Article 8 and 10 factors in assessing whether a RTBF's enforcement was compatible with Article 10.[87] The new list of balancing factors given in *Hurbain* were: 1. *the nature of the information*, 2. *the time*

---

[82] *Lillo-Stenberg and Sæther v Norway* App no 13258/09 (ECHR, 16 January 2014) [97].
[83] See also *Couderc and Hachette Filipacchi Associes v France*, App no 40454/07 (ECHR, 12 June 2014) [84].
[84] Brimblecombe (n 78).
[85] Ibid.
[86] *Hurbain v Belgium* (n 51).
[87] Ibid [214]–[253].

elapsed, 3. *contemporary interest*, 4. *whether the person is well known and their conduct since the events*, 5. *negative repercussions for them*, 6. *degree of accessibility*, 7. *impact on freedom of expression*.[88] It is easy to see how each of these factors could be applied to a RTBF request with respect to personal information online that is false and defamatory. While certain factors elucidated in *Hurbain* should be welcomed, it is argued here that others are less helpful and should only be used by courts with caution (if at all). The factor of the *nature of the information* in question is clearly important and relevant if a RTBF is in dispute (and to the question of the applicability of an exemption such as Article 17(3)(a) UK GDPR). In *Hurbain*, perhaps predictably, the Strasbourg Court considered whether the information was 'sensitive' and falls within the scope of a person's private life or instead the public sphere[89] – this accords with earlier Strasbourg precedent in privacy cases, such as the famous cases of *Von Hannover*. It should be noted that the concept of the RTBF, as least as far as it arises out of the GDPR, does not, in principle, rely on information's sensitivity or 'private nature' – however, in situations which a RTBF is contested in a court (perhaps annexed to a 'defence' or exemption), it is clear that this factor may become relevant. *Hurbain* also raised the importance of the journalistic nature of the material[90] – which, of course, is also relevant to the journalistic defence in the UK GDPR/DPA 2018 and Article 17(3)(a)'s exemption. The Strasbourg Court in *Hurbain* also gave weight to the amount of *time that had elapsed* since the events and the article's publication online.[91] This was particularly relevant as the article in question related to G (a doctor) causing a fatal road traffic accident in 1994.[92] The article was placed in online archives

---

[88] Ibid.
[89] Ibid [214].
[90] Ibid [216].
[91] Ibid [220].
[92] Ibid. See opening matters.

in 2008 and G had been rehabilitated in 2006: the court held that G 'had a legitimate interest, after all that time, in seeking to be allowed to reintegrate into society without being permanently reminded of his past'.[93] While this balancing factor of elapsed time was of clear relevance to *Hurbain* given that the RTBF had been claimed by a rehabilitated, past offender, the passage of time may not always be – and should not always be – a pivotal factor in a RTBF claim. It is important to remember that the spirit of the RTBF is the idea of individual autonomy – that is, that someone can invoke the right because they no longer wish the information to be accessible on the web – to which the length of time is a factor that may *not* be relevant.[94] Indeed, if one was to find that a RTBF was only accessible to (for example) online posts detailing matters of the distant past in a general fashion, the right would be too narrowly constrained – and clearly would not align with the intentions of the EU drafters of Article 17. It is important to raise caveat here to say that in cases involving *past criminal behaviour* (such as in *Hurbain* itself), this factor may well be a legitimate consideration, due in part to the concept of rehabilitation of offenders. It is merely submitted here that this time factor ought not to be encouraged to grow and apply to all RTBF litigation *more generally*, to a range of different factual scenarios. The Grand Chamber in *Hurbain* also delivered precedent pertaining to the concept of the public interest in the context of RTBF claims; this is helpful as this matter has not been clarified by the UK GDPR, DPA 2018 nor subsequent English case law. *Hurbain* states: 'the public interest relates to matters which affect the public to such an extent that it may legitimately take an interest in them, which attract its attention or which concern it to a significant degree, *especially*

---

[93] Ibid [220]–[221].
[94] Ibid. As is the spirit behind the slew of 'rights of the data subject' present in the GDPR, Articles 12–23.

in that they affect the well-being of citizens or the life of the community'.[95] The court went on to elaborate that such an interest would arise if the matter was an important 'social issue',[96] and that public interest is not merely the same thing as the public's 'thirst'[97] for information about people's personal lives. The court then noted that the concept of the public interest would not always be 'decisive', as the concept's applicability can wane or change over time.[98] This is interesting, as it perhaps marks a point of departure from the Strasbourg conception of a RTBF and that arising out of Article 17 UK GDPR. It is argued here that the public interest *is* likely to be a determinative factor in future English RTBF litigation concerning the application of Article 17(3)(a)'s freedom-of-expression exemption. Indeed, it is likely already a latent decisive factor employed by in-house legal teams assessing whether a data subject's RTBF request is upheld. This is because the concept of the public interest enjoys a place of pivotal importance in English privacy jurisprudence with regard to misuse of private information case law. The comparison between RTBF claims and misuse of private information jurisprudence in the English jurisdiction cannot be ignored – one will doubtless have influence on the other.[99] It will be of great interest to lawyers in this area to see how the concept of the public interest is shaped in relation to contentious RTBF claims in the future, particularly in the English jurisdiction. Finally, in *Hurbain*, the court considered the *conduct* of the RTBF subject relevant to whether the right

---

[95] Ibid [223].
[96] Ibid.
[97] Ibid.
[98] Ibid [224].
[99] For discussion of one's influence over the other generally, see Fiona Brimblecombe and Helen Fenwick, 'Keeping control of personal information in the digital age: Efficacy and equivalence of tortious and GDPR/DPA relief?' (2022) 138 Law Quarterly Review 456–80.

ought to be upheld in accordance with the Convention. The ECtHR noted that 'there is nothing to suggest that G. made contact with the media in order to publicise his situation ... on the contrary, all the steps taken by him demonstrate a desire to stay out of the media spotlight'.[100] This is the concept of 'waiver'; the idea that a claimant (often, in privacy law) can waive their privacy rights of the future by previous solicitation of publicity. The factor has been utilized at times by the English courts to block access to redress for invasions of privacy by the press. This factor is problematic for one key reason: that it ignores the agency of the given claimant in asserting their privacy interests on the later occasion, given that some information may be more private than others – and also the idea that a person can change their mind or their feelings about the degree to which they want their personal information to be a matter of public knowledge. This author has criticized this factor's employment in judicial reasoning elsewhere,[101] and it is disappointing to see its echoes in *Hurbain*, even faintly. As can be seen from the critique given here, there is more work still to do in improving and clarifying relevant factors to be used when deciding RTBF claims. This is unsurprising, as the right is, after all, young.

Turning back to the notion of decision makers themselves, unlike the RTBF, in defamation law the adjudicators of an action are solely the English judiciary (and not online 'controllers'). Although undoubtedly experts on the law, Chapter 3 has shown that there is much work the judiciary must do to effectively protect claimants against the rise of online defamation. The Defamation Act 2013 worked to impede the expansion of defamation law at a crucial time when more protection was needed to combat against increased infringements of reputation online. Set in this context of

---

[100] *Hurbain v Belgium* (n 51).
[101] See Brimblecombe and Phillipson (n 61) Part V, D.

judicial apathy, there is no advantage to claimants in a matter being adjudicated traditionally in court (in defamation law) when compared with assessment by a data controller on receipt of a RTBF request. That being said, there are, of course, legitimate concerns about the level of power and responsibility vested in data controllers, which are often private companies, when assessing a RTBF: as Ambrose observes, this 'places a huge, huge burden on them but also gives them a lot of power'.[102] However, with current judicial and legislative trends narrowing successful defamation suits, as demonstrated by Chapter 3, there is no more reason to fear adjudication by a private company than by the English judiciary in the case of online defamation.

IV. Ex post *remedies*

Both defamation law and the RTBF offer *ex post* remedies, in the sense that neither Article 17 nor libel law currently operates a mechanism to prohibit reputationally damaging falsities initially being uploaded to the internet. Rather, both seek to combat this issue after disclosure has occurred. As argued, in the event a potentially defamatory statement has been made online, the RTBF will often afford a timelier solution for the information's removal than litigation in defamation law. A long-standing common law rule forbids the issuing of interim injunctions in defamation in most

---

[102] Meg Leta Ambrose, Georgetown University. See James Doubek, 'Google has received 650,000 "right to be forgotten" requests since 2014' (*NPR*, 28 February 2018) www.npr.org/sections/thetwo-way/2018/02/28/589411543/google-received-650-000-right-to-be-forgotten-requests-since-2014 accessed 26 January 2025. 'EU Court tells Google that people have "the right to be forgotten"' (*NPR*, 13 May 2014) www.npr.org/2014/05/13/312197640/eu-court-tells-google-that-people-have-the-right-to-be-forgotten accessed 24 July 2025.

circumstances,[103] unlike defamation law's sister tort: misuse of private information. It has been argued elsewhere by this author that interim injunctions should be read-in to Article 17 by members of the judiciary in order that they apply to RTBF requests.[104] The tort of misuse of private information and data protection law have sufficiently converged in the English legal system for this to be done, due to the fact they are often considered in tandem in case law; the misuse tort having influence and effect on how the UK GDPR is interpreted in this sense.[105] This argument could (and should) be made by entrepreneurial counsel to best protect personality interests on the web. Further, if this argument *is* accepted in future, the RTBF will cease to operate as an *ex post* remedy – but will also have the force of providing an initial injunction much like the misuse tort, something that defamation law does not provide.

It also must be noted that under Article 17 a data subject can request erasure of their personal data from a secure database *outside of the public domain*. There is always the potential for a database that is initially private to later become public – so, in certain limited circumstances, the RTBF does not solely operate as an *ex post* remedy and can work in these cases to prevent later disclosures of personal (and potentially defamatory) information.

V. The 'right to be forgotten' and the data-dissemination scenarios

It is important to turn to the *data-dissemination* scenarios outlined at the beginning of this book and look at how a claimant in each particular scenario might fare differently when

---

[103] In most circumstances. See Gavin Phillipson, 'The "global pariah", the Defamation Bill and the Human Rights Act' (2012) 63(1) *Northern Ireland Legal Quarterly* 149, 155.

[104] Brimblecombe and Fenwick (n 99) 456.

[105] Ibid.

claiming a RTBF rather than taking action via defamation law. In the *defamation by social media* scenario, for a claimant to assert their rights under Article 17 they need only write to the data controller to demand the information's erasure. This could be a large company such as Facebook or X, or a smaller social media website. As outlined, the definition of data controller in Article 4 UK GDPR is so broad that a website operator or the defamatory information's poster could be classed as a controller; a data subject would be free to write to either.[106] As social media websites are providing a service to users in the UK, the UK GDPR will have extraterritorial effect (even if the websites are domiciled elsewhere).[107] As discussed, large social media websites will already have a strategy in place to assess RTBF requests, with a team likely considering certain factors that add to weight to the claim and any exemptions. Similarly, in the *third-party poster* scenario, a defamed individual would be free to assert their RTBF addressed to the host website as a controller, particularly in the event that the third-party poster themselves may be uncontactable. This would be the same if someone was defamed in a 'virtual world'. If a person was defamed by an *AI tool*, the website where this defamatory remark has been made available would likely fall under the Article 4(7) UK GDPR definition of controller, such that a RTBF claim could be made against them; or in the alternative, the AI tool's manufacturer could be deemed as a controller, as they could be seen as the 'body which, alone or jointly with others, determines the purposes and means of the processing of personal data'.[108] If the defamatory remark was repeated over a year later by the same publisher online, this would not bar any claim made under a RTBF: on the contrary, Article 17(2) takes active steps to prevent such a

---

[106] UK GDPR, Article 4(7).
[107] See UK GDPR Article 3(1) and 2(a).
[108] UK GDPR, Article 4(7).

repetition, by requiring that controllers who are subject to a RTBF request to 'take reasonable steps, including technical measures, to inform [other] controllers which are processing the personal data that the data subject has requested the erasure by such controllers of any links to, or copy or replication of, those personal data'.[109] This is strikingly different from the position of English defamation law with s 8.

VI. Future of the 'right to be forgotten' in UK and European law

This chapter has shown that, for a number of different reasons, the RTBF as a route to remedy for defamatory statements posted online has a number of distinct advantages over litigating in defamation law. However, it is important to also state that there is always more that can be done in order to protect personal reputation and dignity in the face of the rapid rise of defamatory remarks made on the web. There have been a number of RTBF-style cases heard at the Strasbourg Court since the CJEU's *Google Spain* decision, most notably *Hurbain*,[110] as already discussed in this chapter, but also the earlier cases of *M.L. and W.W. v Germany* and *Biancardi v Italy*.[111] *Biancardi* was decided in 2021 before the pivotal case of *Hurbain* and was a more modest early foray into establishing a pattern of judicial reasoning, applicable at the Strasbourg Court, to RTBF decisions. The applicant, who was the editor of an online newspaper, had, in 2008, published an article concerning a fight at a restaurant.[112] The applicant was asked by one of the people involved in the fight and the restaurant itself in 2010 to remove the article from the internet, which he did

---

[109] UK GDPR, Article 17(2).

[110] *Hurbain v Belgium* (n 51).

[111] *M.L. and W.W. v Germany* App nos 60798/10 and 65599/10 (28 June 2018). *Biancardi v Italy* App no 77419/16 (25 November 2021).

[112] *Biancardi v Italy* (n 111) [5].

not do.[113] However, at a later hearing in 2011 the applicant admitted that he had de-indexed the article, resulting in it being harder to find.[114] The applicant editor was given a fine in the domestic Italian courts for breaching the claimant's 'reputation' as well as the relevant national law, the Personal Data Protection Code, and this decision was upheld by the domestic Supreme Court.[115] He claimed that his Article 10 rights had been infringed in so doing. The ECtHR, however, found no violation had taken place in *Biancardi*; it is a short judgment at 24 pages, and only 5 of those pages form a substantive assessment of the merits of the case. The court explained that the crux of the matter was the applicant's failure to de-list or de-index the article – and this is what the relevant issue was in the domestic courts.[116] In *Biancardi*, the Strasbourg Court used Article 8–10 – 'balancing factors' elucidated in the 2012 case of *Axel Springer* – as a starting point to assess whether there was a violation of Article 10.[117] This was undoubtedly a misstep, as the factors elucidated in *Axel Springer* more strongly relate to press intrusion into the lives of celebrities by the traditional media, as per the facts of the case (and many other Strasbourg cases that followed).[118] For this reason, these factors are largely outdated and of only limited help when considering Article 8–10 rights and the balance to be struck in RTBF-style claims. A RTBF arising from either *Google Spain* or Article 17 GDPR has a different context and aim to the Strasbourg jurisprudence arising out of the traditional, press intrusion cases of the 1980s, 1990s and 2000s, both in the ECtHR and the English courts. Interestingly, the ECtHR seemed aware that it was following

---

[113] Ibid [8].
[114] Ibid [10].
[115] Ibid [13] and [14].
[116] Ibid [59].
[117] Ibid [61].
[118] See n 59.

the incorrect approach for these very reasons in *Biancardi*;[119] ultimately, *Biancardi* has been superseded by the judgment of *Hurbain* in the Grand Chamber as earlier discussed, which was considerably more detailed in setting out new criteria for assessment in RTBF case law at Strasbourg.

Although the ECtHR's case law has been active, particularly with regard to RTBF requests relating to criminal pasts,[120] the same cannot be said of case law in the English jurisdiction. Aside from *NT1 and NT2* discussed previously,[121] in 2022 there was another English case concerning spent convictions, *ABC*.[122] In *ABC*, the claimant had pled guilty to nine counts of fraud in a Magistrates Court in 2015.[123] The defendant was a journalist and a court reporter, and the matter complained of was a factual, court report of the case on the journalist's blog.[124] The claimant ran a variety of actions against the blog post (including claiming it was misuse of private information and harassment),[125] but most notably argued that she had a 'right to be forgotten' under Article 17 after her convictions became spent in 2017.[126] The Court in *ABC* found it relevant that the claimant 'has not been rehabilitated by her convictions and sentence' as she had asserted her innocence on multiple occasions following her convictions.[127] The blog had been

---

[119] But it did not go as far as rectifying this to elucidate new factors of assessment. See *Biancardi v Italy* (n 111) [63].

[120] Mikel Anderez Belategi, 'The right to be forgotten concerning the criminal past: Developments in the case law of the European Court of Human Rights with particular reference to the anonymisation of digital press archives' (2024) 14(4) *Oñati Socio-Legal Series: The Influence of New Technologies on Law* 1639.

[121] See n 44.

[122] *ABC v Palmer* [2022] EWHC 3128 (KB).

[123] Ibid [2].

[124] Ibid [3].

[125] Ibid [5].

[126] Ibid.

[127] Ibid [49].

taken down permanently in May 2021.[128] However, before this, it was made public again by the defendant between June 2020 and May 2021, but the Court found this fell under the defendant's right to freedom of expression, as the claimant was making false claims about him 'and the events he had witnessed [in the Magistrates Court] at the time', and therefore the GDPR had not been breached.[129] Both *NT1* and *ABC* are low-level decisions, and hardly amount to a flood of caselaw on the RTBF. *ABC* follows *NT1* rather than adds to existing precedent.

There may be a number of reasons for the drought in English RTBF-style case law. Firstly, RTBF requests are often sent by private individuals and then examined and assessed privately by data controllers, who are themselves either private individuals or employees at a large company. On the outcome of such a request, the person who made it may either be satisfied or choose not to take the matter further, perhaps due to reasons supplied by the controller in the event that an erasure request is denied (for example, someone may feel that the public interest may be sufficiently engaged to warrant the request's refusal). This is a private loop and, as such, requires no court involvement – and generates no case law. Secondly, in the case of the UK, the ICO would normally be expected to 'intervene' if an appropriate matter is brought to their door – such as a failure to uphold what appears to be a legitimate erasure request – and partner with a claimant in bringing the matter in question before an English court on the basis of Article 17 UK GDPR. High-profile cases such as these have not happened since the UK GDPR's adoption. It is argued here that the ICO should play a more proactive role in bringing RTBF-style complaints to English courts, helping claimants to assert their erasure rights – particularly in light of the mounting

---

[128] Ibid [81].
[129] Ibid [84]–[85].

problem of online defamation. A more stringent approach in this vein would generate much needed English case law on the matter and give both claimants and potential defendants more information about the detail and precise scope of the right. This is particularly relevant as major reform of the ICO proposed by the then Conservative government in 2024 has since been abandoned, as the Data Protection and Digital Information (DPDI) Bill which included such reform has been 'washed up' and jettisoned in the wake of the 2024 general election, which shifted the UK's governance to a Labour Party majority.[130] More cases brought of this nature would not only potentially vindicate claimants in cases where false and potentially defamatory personal information is posted online, but would also give other individuals considering asserting their rights in this way an idea of what balancing framework the English courts intend to adopt when considering a disputed RTBF claim. More jurisprudence would also add much needed clarity and detail to the rather open-ended drafting of many aspects of Article 17 UK GDPR and how the courts may solve 'hard' cases.

Through involvement with the ICO, a number of test cases could be brought on the basis of a refused erasure request, where the information in question is personal data but also false and potentially defamatory. More precedent would be generated as to whether courts would treat an erasure request differently on the basis that the information was *false*. Strasbourg and English jurisprudence suggests that, in fact, an erasure request made under Article 17 that relates to false personal information about an individual would in fact have a stronger case for erasure than truthful information. This could be covered in the *nature of the information* factor as articulated by *Hurbain*,[131] and the lack of truth in the information contested

---

[130] See the DPDI Bill (No 2) https://bills.parliament.uk/bills/3430 accessed 27 January 2025.

[131] *Hurbain v Belgium* (n 51) [215]–[253].

for removal would likely not have requisite 'contemporary interest' as per *Hurbain*,[132] nor perhaps the public interest value pertaining to Article 17(3)(a) UK GDPR, as it may be difficult to argue that the public have a pressing need to know untrue information. Indeed, in *Google Spain* itself, the fact the continued access to the (truthful) information gave an inaccurate impression of the claimant was a powerful argument; the CJEU found that under Articles 6, 12 and 14 of the DPD '95 that data must be adequate, relevant, as well as accurate and up to date, and not 'irrelevant' or 'excessive'.[133] Although this case was decided under the previous EU data protection law framework, it is clear that the accuracy of personal data online is still a paramount concern of the GDPR. Article 16 UK GDPR contains 'the right to rectification', which requires that data subjects 'have the right to obtain from the controller without undue delay the rectification of inaccurate personal data concerning him or her'.[134] The relevance of Article 16 may also work to bolster a RTBF request regarding untrue defamatory content online, much like a claim in misuse of private information is supported by the presence of breach of confidence elements in an action.[135] In the event that a RTBF claim is refused, then a claimant could potentially invoke Article 16's rectification right to amend false and defamatory personal data on the web. This may go some way to dispel defamatory imputations conveyed by a given post. Complete erasure of such a statement, rather than mere rectification, in many cases, may, however, be the preferred remedy due to the binary nature of such statements.[136]

---

[132] Ibid.

[133] See Article 6, Directive 95/46/EC (n 6) and *Google Spain* (n 7) [92] and [94].

[134] UK GDPR, Article 16(1).

[135] As was the case in *HRH Prince of Wales v Associated Newspapers* [2006] EWCA Civ 1776 and *McKennit v Ash* [2006] EWCA CIV 1714.

[136] On the topic of 'complete erasure', it should be noted that the CJEU have made it clear that a RTBF order will, often, only be applicable to

The final issue that must be discussed here is the future of UK data protection law more broadly stated. As the UK left the EU after Brexit, the UK GDPR now has the status of domestic law, much like the DPA 2018, and is therefore vulnerable to amendments by successive governments and legislatures. Despite only being in force since 2018, the Conservative government incumbent during this period was at pains to alter the UK GDPR in order to remedy what many party members felt were unduly strict rules on both large and small businesses in terms of GDPR compliance. This was despite the fact that, by 2024, many businesses had already installed data-protection compliance officers and developed procedures in order to act in accordance with GDPR rules. In the wake of an earlier unsuccessful attempt to amend UK data protection law under Boris Johnson,[137] the second DPDI Bill proposed by the later iteration of the Conservative government was nearing its final stages when Rishi Sunak called a general election for 4 July 2024.[138] As a result of this, the Bill ran out of time to pass through the legislative houses and was never enacted. The washed-up DPDI (No 2) Bill proposed several changes to the UK GDPR and the DPA 2018, which could be seen as 'tinkering' around the edges of data protection law in order to reduce the overall protections offered. The idea behind the Bill was that it would reduce burdens for compliance on small businesses and make it easier to conduct aspects of scientific research. The Bill's primary changes were to reduce

---

the EU – although it acknowledged the possibility of a court ordering a worldwide de-referencing order in future under the GDPR. See C-507/17 *Google LLC v CNIL* ECLI:EU:C:2019:772 [72] and Cathryn Hopkins, 'Territorial scope in recent CJEU cases: *Google v CNIL / Glawischnig-Piesczek v Facebook*' (*Inforrm*, 9 November 2019) https://inforrm.org/2019/11/09/territorial-scope-in-recent-cjeu-cases-google-v-cnil-glawischnig-piesczek-v-facebook-cathryn-hopkins/ accessed 23 May 2025.

[137] DPDI Bill (No 1) https://bills.parliament.uk/bills/3322 accessed 27 January 2025.

[138] DPDI Bill (No 2) (n 130).

the burden on data controllers in order to relax rules around record keeping, alter the operation of data protection officers at companies, change GDPR impact assessments, broaden the scope of scientific research and, perhaps most concerningly, change the definition of 'personal data' in order to narrow it – and therefore narrow the amount of processing to which the UK GDPR would apply.[139] Ultimately, this Bill never came into force. Since the Labour Party's success in the 2024 UK general election, a new data protection Act has been very recently been passed: the Data (Use and Access) Act 2025, under Labour's initiative.[140] The Act is considerably less far-reaching and less punitive than the earlier DPDI (No 2) Bill and does not change the UK data protection law framework anywhere near as significantly (although one could argue that the proposed DPDI (No 2) changes were not particularly momentous anyway). Legal experts have observed that the changes in the Data (Use and Access) Act are only 'incremental' and do not represent a significant change to the law as it stands.[141] The changes in the 2025 Act (then a Bill) have also altered on its passage through the legislative process.[142] The Data (Use and Access) Act chiefly adopts a 'smart data' model,[143] and proposes some comparatively more

---

[139] Ibid.

[140] See https://bills.parliament.uk/bills/3825 accessed 25 May 2025.

[141] Nathalie Moreno and Ben Pumphrey, 'Empowering data use, access, and sharing across the UK's digital economy' (*Kennedys Law*, 30 October 2024) https://kennedyslaw.com/en/thought-leadership/article/2024/the-new-data-use-and-access-bill-empowering-data-use-access-and-sharing-across-the-uks-digital-economy/ accessed 27 January 2025.

[142] https://bills.parliament.uk/bills/3825/publications and see Nathalie Moreno, 'The UK's Data (Use and Access) Bill: Latest amendments and legal implications' (*Kennedys Law*, 6 March 2025) https://kennedyslaw.com/en/thought-leadership/article/2025/the-uks-data-use-and-access-bill-latest-amendments-and-legal-implications/ accessed 25 May 2025.

[143] See Explanatory Notes to the Data (Use and Access) Bill [HL] 9 [2] https://publications.parliament.uk/pa/bills/cbill/59-01/0179/en/240179en.pdf accessed 25 May 2025.

modest changes to the UK's ICO (which will still remain independent),[144] while attempting to balance innovation with strong data protection ideals. The Act will create a new lawful ground of data processing under Article 6(ea) UK GDPR, 'processing is necessary for the purposes of a recognised legitimate interest'.[145] These interests are specified in Annex 1 to the Act.[146] Most controversially, the new Act also allows the government (Secretary of State) to update this list by regulation, contingent on parliament's approval.[147] This effectively gives the government the ability to expand this list at will (subject to parliamentary intervention), therefore rendering more types of data processing lawful in so doing. If this list were to rapidly expand in future, it may in practice work to reduce the number of scenarios in which a data subject can argue for a RTBF on the basis that data has been *unlawfully processed* under Article 17(1)(d). However, this is not a significant cause for concern, as a data subject could instead argue that it is *no longer necessary* for the data to be processed under Article 17(1)(a), or instead object to its processing on the grounds of Article 17(1)(c),

---

[144] Research briefing, Data (Use and Access) Bill https://lordslibrary.parliament.uk/research-briefings/lln-2024-0063/ and see 'Information Commissioner's response to the Data (Use and Access) (DUA) Bill' https://ico.org.uk/about-the-ico/the-data-use-and-access-dua-bill/information-commissioner-s-response-to-the-data-use-and-access-bill/ (both accessed 27 January 2025). Also see Explanatory Notes (n 134). Also see Department for Science, Innovation and Technology, 'Guidance Data (Use and Access) Act factsheet: ICO' (27 June 2025) accessible at: https://www.gov.uk/government/publications/data-use-and-access-act-2025-factsheets/data-use-and-access-act-factsheet-ico

[145] Moreno and Pumphrey (n 132) and Data (Use and Access) Act 2025, clause 70(2)(b). Also see Schedule 4, Annex 1, 'Lawfulness of processing: Recognised legitimate interests', which lists the recognized legitimate interests. The Act is available at: https://www.legislation.gov.uk/ukpga/2025/18/enacted#schedule-4 (last accessed 23/7/25).

[146] Schedule 4, Annex 1, Data (Use and Access) Act 2025 (n 136).

[147] Data (Use and Access) Act 2025, clause 70(4)(6). Also see Explanatory Notes (n 134) 73, part 546.

or perhaps withdraw consent to the information's processing according to Article 17(1)(b) UK GDPR, any of which would render a RTBF functional. Furthermore, this may not be cause for concern regardless, as any governmental expansion to this list of recognized legitimate interests would be subject to parliamentary approval and under Annex 1 of the Act, this list is narrow. It appears, then, that the RTBF will not suffer from these changes to the law. This is perhaps not surprising, as the current Labour government will wish to maintain the UK's current adequacy rating from the EU in terms of data protection law, as this is necessary for it to conduct business with the EU. The EU's current adequacy decision for the UK is set to be reviewed in December 2025.[148] There have also been political rumours circulating for quite some time that certain members of the Labour Party wish the UK to eventually rejoin the EU,[149] or at the very least negotiate a substantial trade deal with the single market, resulting in complex treaties drawn up that may include compliance with the EU's data protection standards as a necessity. In any event, if at some point a comprehensive change to the UK's data protection framework is undertaken to the detriment of the RTBF, the Strasbourg Court has acknowledged that it recognizes the RTBF of individuals in some circumstances under Article 8.[150] The UK continues to accede to the ECHR and is bound by rulings of the ECtHR – English courts have an interpretive obligation to read English law in light of the Convention.[151]

---

[148] ICO, 'Adequacy' https://ico.org.uk/for-organisations/data-protection-and-the-eu/data-protection-and-the-eu-in-detail/adequacy/ accessed 23 July 2025.

[149] William Keegan, 'Keir Starmer ruled out rejoining the EU: Now he must think again' *The Guardian* (7 July 2024) www.theguardian.com/business/article/2024/jul/07/keir-starmer-ruled-out-rejoining-the-eu-now-he-must-think-again accessed 27 January 2025.

[150] *Hurbain v Belgium* (n 51) [199] 68.

[151] See ss 2, 3 and 6(1) of the Human Rights Act 1998.

As such, it appears that the RTBF is here to stay. While any changes to the RTBF are unwelcome from the perspective of the advocates of personality rights (and this book), Article 17 UK GDPR's vulnerability to legislative change is, of course, something it shares with English defamation law.

★★★

Conclusion for Chapter 4

Through a process of direct comparison of defamation law and Article 17 UK GDPR, this chapter has argued that the RTBF provides, in many cases, a more effective route to redress for those defamed on the internet. It is a more simplistic remedy in terms of the action needed to be taken on the part of those defamed and is also more accessible than a lengthy action in defamation law as it is easier to understand and considerably more affordable for data subjects. While defamation law is technically complex, the substantial media attention afforded to the RTBF is something that many people are now aware of, in the wake of *Google Spain*. The legal hurdles that must be overcome to assert a RTBF are far fewer than in defamation law. In every *data-dissemination* scenario that has been considered by this book, the RTBF provides a more straightforward route to an ultimate remedy than English defamation law. Despite this, the RTBF is not a perfect solution. This chapter has made it clear that more English case law on this topic is needed to accurately ascertain some of the details of Article 17 and how it must be balanced against freedom of expression in challenging cases. It is suggested here that, in future, online defamation claims ought to be run in tandem with RTBF actions in the event that an erasure request has been refused; in this way, legal observers can see how both regimes may impact one another when considered with regard to the same issue. Finally, it is stressed that any significant statutory change to the RTBF in Article

17 UK GDPR is most unwelcome from the perspective of upholding rigorous protection of reputation and therefore personal dignity, in the wake of more defamatory information on the internet circa 2025 than ever before.

Conclusion

This book has argued that the law must do more to protect those defamed on the internet. By considering English defamation law using a number of different '*data-dissemination* scenarios', it has argued that the law is currently deficient in safeguarding against the rise in defamatory content posted to the web. In making this argument, Chapter 1 considered the technological shift that has taken place in society, transforming the UK into a truly digital world. Cloud computing has made this shift possible, enabling websites to grow exponentially, storing and transmitting vast amounts of information – including personal data. Social media usage is now societally acceptable and even expected, with individuals posting potentially defamatory content about others at a click of a button. Perhaps the most prevailing threat to reputation circa 2025 is that posed by artificial intelligence (AI)-powered technologies. The disturbing creation of 'deepfakes' poses a particularly significant reputational threat. This monograph then evaluated the philosophical underpinnings of reputation and concluded that the fundamental human interest that reputation safeguards is personal dignity (including self-perception). This is the interest that is violated when a defamatory statement about an individual is publicized online. Chapter 3, Part I demonstrated that far from protecting those defamed online, the reform of the Defamation Act 2013 has resulted in new obstacles for those seeking redress under English defamation law. The s 1 'serious harm' threshold raises the bar for all claimants in defamation, but particularly negatively affects those defamed online when arguing an 'inferential' case. Section 8's one-year limitation period for the repetition of defamatory statements by the same publisher impedes claimants in bringing a second action over material that is in substantially the same form, at a time when more (not less) litigation in libel law is necessary to combat reputationally damaging statements on the web. Chapter 3, Part II moved to discuss online phenomena, such as the s 5 defence for host websites and the risk to reputational harm rendered by advancements in AI. Finally, Chapter 4 argued that the 'right to be forgotten' (RTBF) in Article 17 of the UK General Data Protection Regulation (GDPR) presents a more comprehensive and effective route to redress than that presently offered by English defamation law. This is due to the RTBF's ease, speed, lack of reliance on the court system and breadth, encompassing many different online defamation scenarios. It is important to finish with a warning. It is crucial that academics, practitioners and politicians realize the considerable threat to reputation and personal dignity that online technologies pose. For this reason, the RTBF must be safeguarded in the UK's legal system, as it represents one of the few current ways a balance between freedom of expression and individual reputation can be restored online. This is particularly pertinent as the UK GDPR is now vulnerable to legislative change after Brexit. The right is a safe haven for those defamed on the web and it must be given the space to flourish.

Index

References to notes show both the page number
and the note number (24n74).

A

Aaronson v Stones 13
ABC v Palmer 172–3
affordable technology 16, 18–21
'AI Act' (European Union) 125
AI tool manufacturers 128, 130–1, 135–6, 137, 169
Albright, Dallin 122, 126, 129n273
Alpin, Tanya 56
Ambrose, Meg Leta 167
American defamation law *see* US defamation law
Amersi v Leslie 76, 77
Ames v Spamhaus Project Ltd 71
Apple 5n3, 26
archives, online 99, 163–4
artificial intelligence (AI) 2, 6, 28–31, 34–5, 182, 183
  'hallucinates' and creates false information about living people when responding to text prompts 107
  and reputational threat 31–3
  see also defamation by AI tool or virtual world scenario
augmented reality 26–8, 34, 62, 133
avatars 24, 25, 26, 34, 62
Axel Springer AG v Germany 157, 171

B

balancing exercise 44–5, 161–4
Banks v Cadwalladr 84, 91, 155
Biancardi v Italy 170–2

Bing, and ChatGPT 123–4
Blake v Fox 2–3, 13, 82, 84, 87
blockchain technology 133
Bosland, Jason 56
British Chiropractic Association v Singh 87
Bukhari v Bukhari 80

C

Caliskan, Aylin 123, 124, 128, 130n279
Campbell v MGN Ltd 157
character.ai 29, 62
Charter of Fundamental Rights of the European Union 143
chatbots 6, 29–30, 32–2, 34–5, 62
ChatGPT-2 122
ChatGPT-3 122
ChatGPT-4 2, 123–4
Cheong, Ben Chester 25, 26
Cheong, Inyoung 123, 124, 128, 130n279
Christianity 39, 40
Cicero 39, 40
citizen journalists 156, 159
cloud computing 7–10, 34, 182
Coker v Nwakanma 74
Communications Decency Act (US) 109, 127
competing expression interest 162
'contributor immunity' 90
Cooke v MGN Ltd 71
Cooley, Charles 41, 51
Courtney v Ronksley 67–8
Court of Appeal 71–2, 84

INDEX

Court of Justice of the European Union (CJEU) 142, 143–4, 153, 155, 159, 175
Craik, Kenneth H. 54

D

Data (Use and Access) Act 135, 177–9
data controller 149–51, 152, 153, 156, 158, 160
  definition 169
  and balancing exercise 161, 162
  concerns about the level of power and responsibility vested in 167
  and DPDI (No 2) Bill 177
  and repetition of statements online over a year later scenario 170
data-dissemination scenarios 60–3, 168–70
Data Protection 1995 (DPD '95) 142, 143, 144, 159, 170–2, 175
deepfakes 30–2, 35, 62, 131–6, 137, 182
deep learning 132
Defamation Act 2013 3–4, 44, 166, 182–3
  abolished the common law rule of *Brunswick v Harmer* 63
  and defamation by social media scenario 61
  prioritizes freedom of expression at the expense of reputation 138
  and 'publication on matter of public interest' defence 160
  see also serious harm threshold; single publication rule; websites, defence for operators of under s 5 Defamation Act 2013
defamation by AI tool or virtual world scenario 62–3, 136–7, 140
  and Article 17 GDPR 150
  and deepfakes and defamation 131–6

nature of the threat 123–5
rising threat 120–3
and RTBF 169
who should be responsible for an AI tool's defamatory speech? 125–31
defamation by social media scenario 60–1, 92–4, 105, 107, 140
  and Article 17 GDPR 149
  Article 17 GDPR 169
  and 'domestic purposes' exemption 157–8
defamation law 37, 38
  and dignity 39–46
  and honour 46–8
  hurdles to making a claim 155–6, 160
  and sociality theory 53–8
defamatory statements 2–3, 19, 20, 21, 54, 68–9, 110, 155
  and AI 107, 122, 123, 125, 126, 128
  and avatars 62
  and *Delfi* 115
  and Facebook 76
  and GDPR 154, 167, 170
  and libraries 99
  and multiple publication rule 94
  and one-year limitation period 182–3
  and repetition of statements online over a year later scenario 63, 66
  and republication in 'substantially the same' form 101
  and serious harm threshold 50, 67
  and single publication rule 95
  and social ties 57, 58
  and Strębska 51
  and third-party poster scenario 111
defence of fair comment 86, 87
Delfi AS v Estonia 112–15, 116, 117, 118, 119, 120

Denman v Associated Newspapers Ltd 104
De Scandalis Magnatum 47
Descheemaeker, Eric 44
dignity 50, 58, 86, 182, 183
   definitions 42–4, 58–9
   and balancing rights 44–6
   conceptualizing 40–2
   culture 41
   history 39–40
   and reputation 48
'disruptive technology' 28
'domestic purposes' exemption 157
DPDI (No 2) Bill 176–7
droit l'oubli (a right to erasure) 142
duelling 47
Duke of Brunswick v Harmer 63, 66, 94–5
Dyson v Channel 4 51
Dyson v MGN Ltd 87

E

Eady, Sir David 104
Ecclesiastical Courts 37
Economou v de Frietas 90
Edward I 37
emotional harm 136
engagement metrics 80, 81
Erdos, David 75
European Convention on Human Rights (ECHR) 56
   Article 8 97, 157, 162, 179
   Article 10 3–4, 69, 97, 110, 117, 157
European Court of Human Rights (ECtHR) 155, 179
   Biancardi v Italy 171–2
   Hurbain v Belgium 161–6
   Karako v Hungary 52–3
   on dignity 39, 45
   Pfeifer v Austria 56
   and websites, defence for operators of under s 5 Defamaetion Act 2013 112–20

European Union (EU)
   'AI Act' 125
   Charter of Fundamental Rights of the European Union 143

F

'face' 56
   culture 41
Facebook 11, 14, 20, 76, 111, 119
   3,049 billion active users worldwide 1
   deposed Myspace 12
   and 'Facemash' 8
   and *Stocker v Stocker* 13, 83
fair comment, defence of 86, 87
Ferdinand v MGN 157
First Amendment 97
Firth v State 97–8
Fleming, John 39
'floodgates' argument 98, 128–9
Flood v Times Newspapers 14
Forbes, and the Metaverse 23
France
   and *droit l'oubli* (a right to erasure) 142
   Press Law 58
freedom of expression 67–8, 116, 138, 156, 183
freedom of speech 62, 97

G

Gambin et al. 133
Gearty, Conor 44, 45
General Data Protection Regulation (GDPR) 25, 140–1, 145–9, 176–80, 183
   and accessibility of redress 149–53
   background context 141–4
   and data-dissemination scenarios 168–70
   and decision making 160–7
   and defamation law 153–60
   and *ex post* remedies 167–8
   and personal data 175

INDEX

Generation Z, and 'skim reading' 17
Goldsmith v Bissett-Powell 77, 111
Google 29, 33, 151, 153, 159, 160
Google Glass 27
Google Spain SL and Another v Agencia Española de protección de Datos (AEPD) and Another 142, 143–4, 153, 159, 175
Guardian News and Media Ltd 56

H

hallucinations, and AI 107, 123–4, 125, 130, 131
Handforth parish council meeting 19
Harder, Amy 97, 98, 99
Hashimoto, Tatsunori 128, 130
hate speech 115–16, 118
Hayden v Family Education Trust 80–1
Hay v Cresswell 13, 90–1
Hemming v Poulton 104–5
Henderson, Peter 128, 130
home working 16
honest opinion 86, 87, 156
honour 46–8
Howarth, David 41–2, 50, 53, 54, 55–6
Hunt, Earl B. 29
Hurbain v Belgium 162–6, 170, 174–5
'hybrid' working policy 16
Hyde, Richard 69–70

I

Iglesias, Teresa 54
image-based social media websites 12–13
'incorporeal property' 48
inferential case 73, 74, 78–9, 82, 105, 182
Information Commissioner's Officer (ICO) 152, 173, 178
injuria 13, 37

Instagram 12–13
interim injunctions 110, 167–8

J

Jameel (Youssef) v Dow Jones & Co Inc 69, 72
Jameel v Wall Street Journal 88
Jočinė, Judge 52–3
journalism, responsible 87–90
journalistic exemption 158–9, 163

K

Kant, Immanuel 39–40
Karako v Hungary 45, 52–3
Karasavva, Vasileia 132, 136
Kay, Mr Justice 87
Kerr, Lord 83–4
Killmister, Suzy 43
King's Courts 37
Kohno, Tadayoshi 123, 124, 128, 130n279
Kolani, Aurel 41
Kumar, Sapna 102

L

Lachaux v Independent Print Ltd and Another 24n74, 52, 71–4, 78
LaMDA, and AI chatbot 29
language models 122–3
large language models (LLMs) 123–4, 125, 138
laundering, social media 133
legal personality 126, 128
Lemley, Mark 128, 130
Lemoine, Blake 29
libel 10, 67, 68, 87, 100, 155
 and *ex post* remedies 167
 and *Hemming v Poulton* 104
 and OpenAI 123
 and presumption-of-damage principle 73
 and Privy Council 96
 and property theory 49
 and psychological integrity 45
 and slander 24, 70

libellus famosus 37
Libel Reform Campaign 88, 89
libraries, and defamation suits 99
Limitation Act, s 32A 104–5
looking-glass self theory 50–3, 56

M

machine learning 2, 33, 62
Magyar Tartalomszolgaltatok Egyesulete v Hungary 112–13, 116–17
Mail Online 106
Mayer-Schonberger, Viktor 7
McCrudden, Christopher 43
McNamara, Laurence 49
Mead, George Herbert 41
Meta 6, 22, 23, 111
Metaverse 6–7, 22–3, 24, 25
Miller, Power v Turner 81, 84
misuse of private information tort 168
MIT, and 'Detect Fakes' 31
M.L. and W.W. v Germany 170
Monroe v Hopkins 71, 84–5
Mullender, Professor Richard 51
Mullis, Alistair 44, 45
multiple jurisdiction issue 100
multiple publication rule 63, 94
Musk, Elon 18
Myspace 11, 12

N

Neu, Jerome 58
newspaper websites 106
NFTs (non-fungible tokens), and the Metaverse 22
Nicholls, Lord 84, 88
Noorbhai, Aalia 132, 136
NT1 and NT2 v Google LLC (Intervenor: The Information Commissioner) 159, 173

O

Old Testament, and dignity 39
onlife 30
online archives 99, 163–4
Online Safety Act 134–5
online worlds 21–6
OpenAI 123
Oppitz, Marcus 8
ostracism, social 55–6

P

Packham v Wightman 82
personal data
  'domestic purposes' exemption 157
  and DPDI (No 2) Bill 177
  and social media 2
  and the UK GDPR 154, 175
Personal Data Protection Code (Italy) 171
personal dignity 86, 182, 183
personal integrity 52
personality rights as property 48–50
Pfeifer v Austria 56
Phillipson, Gavin 100–1, 102
PJS (Appellant) v News Group Newspapers Ltd (Respondent) 157
Pokemon GO 26–7
pornography, deepfake 31, 132, 134, 135
Post, Robert 48, 53, 54, 55, 57, 58n113
  on dignity 58n114
  on honour 46–7
Pound, Roscoe 48
predictive text models 122
presumption-of-damage principle 73
pretrained generative model on the whole internet AI program 122
private self 41
Privy Council 95–6
property, and personality rights 48–50
psychological integrity 45
public interest 86, 88–9, 130–1, 160, 164–5
public self 41

INDEX

public's right to know 88
Pufendorf, Samuel von 40

R

repetition of statements online over a year later scenario 63, 66, 101–2, 103–4, 105–6, 169–70
reputation
 and community bonds 54
 damage to 10
 defamation law attempts to protect 38
 and dignity 39
 and freedom of expression 138
 and *Karako v Hungary* 52–3
 and personality rights as property 48–9, 50
 and social media 13–15
 theories 59
 threat to 24–6, 27–8, 31–3, 182, 183
Reynolds defence of responsible journalism at common law 86, 156
Reynolds v Times Newspapers 84, 87–8
Rhodes v OPO and Another 136
Rice, Mrs Justice Collins 84
right to be forgotten (RTBF) 140, 183
 and accessibility of redress 149–53
 and Article 17 GDPR 145–9, 175, 180–1
 background context 141–4
 and Data (Use and Access) Act 178–9
 and data-dissemination scenarios 168–70
 and decision making 160–7
 and *ex post* remedies 167–8
 and future of in UK law 172–4
 and hurdles to making a claim 153–60
'right to criticise' 162
'right to erasure' 144
 see also right to be forgotten (RTBF)
right to know 88
Riley v Murray 2–3, 82
'role model argument' 162
Roman laws 37
Rooney, Coleen 152
Rosen, Michael 43
Rousseau, Jean-Jacques 40
Ruparelia, Nayan B. 8, 9

S

Sample, Ian 30n100
Sanchez v France 117–19, 120
Sancinito, Jane 48–9, 54, 55n96
satellite internet connection 17–18
Scott, Andrew 44, 45
Second Restatement of Torts (US) 97
self-esteem 51, 52, 56
semi-autonomous production AI program 122
Serafin v Malkiewicz 89
serious harm threshold 24, 58, 105, 139
 background 67–70
 how does one evidence serious harm caused or likely to be caused by an online post? 75–9
 is there a different approach to s 1 where the internet is concerned? 83–6
 new s 1 threshold 70–5
 Section 1's introduction in the context of the codified defences in the 2013 Act 86–91
 what is the significance of viewership and engagement metrics to s 1? 79–83
Sewell, Charlie 68, 69
Sexual Offences Act 135
single publication rule 95, 140
 background to s 8 94–8
 mitigating factor: s 32A of the Limitation Act 1980 103–5

thin justifications 98–101
what is republication in 'substantially the same' form? 101–3
'skim reading' 17
slander 24, 70
smart contracts 133
smartphones 15, 16
Snapchat 12–13, 26
sociality theory 53–8
social media 1–2, 6, 34
  birth of 11–13
  and augmented reality 26
  laundering 133
  and threats to reputation 13–15
  see also Facebook; X (formerly Twitter)
social ostracism 55–6
social ties 57–8
societal cloud 9
Socrates 51
Star Chamber 37, 47
Starlink 17–18
Starmer, Keir 1
Steyn, Mrs Justice 155
Stocker v Stocker 13, 48, 83
Strasbourg Court *see* European Court of Human Rights (ECtHR)
Strębska, Katarzyna 41, 51, 56
strong ties 57
Sumption, Lord 24n74, 72–4
Supreme Court (UK)
  Guardian News and Media Ltd 56
  Lachaux v Independent Print Ltd and Another 51–2, 72–4
  Serafin v Malkiewicz 89
  Stocker v Stocker 47–8, 83

T

technology, affordable 16, 18–21
third-party poster scenario 61–2, 107–9, 111, 136–7, 169
Thornton v Telegraph Media Group 69, 72
ties, social 57–8

TikTok 12–13, 15, 77–8
Tomsu, Peter 8
tort of misuse of private information 168
transactional transparency 133
trial waiting times 150
truth defence 86
Twitter/X *see* X (formerly Twitter)

U

ubiquitous computing 8
Ukraine, and Starlink 18
Uniform Single Publication Act (US) 97
US defamation law 97–8, 100, 101
  Communications Decency Act 109, 127
  Second Restatement of Torts 97
  Uniform Single Publication Act 97
US Supreme Court 39

V

Van Vechten Veeder, Coles 38, 70
Vardy, Rebekah 152
Vardy v Rooney 2–3, 152
Vertucci et al 28
video-based social media websites 12–13
virtual worlds 22, 23, 62, 120
Vizetelly v Mudie's Select Library 99
Volokh, Eugene 121–2, 123–4, 130
Von Hannover v Germany 157, 163
VRChat 23

W

'Wagatha Christie' defamation litigation 151, 152
Wainwright v Home Office 136
'waiver' 166
Waldron, Jeremy 42, 46
Warby, Lord Justice 71, 72, 76–7, 79, 95, 159
weak ties 57

websites, defence for operators of under s 5 Defamation Act 2013 14, 21, 137
  approach of the Strasbourg Court 112–20
  new defence 107–9
  potential issues 110–11
Westminster Printing Press 37
Whitfield, John 55n93
Wilkinson v Downton 136
Wilson, Lord 89
Wood, Lori A. 100
Wright v Granath 81

X

X (formerly Twitter) 2, 15, 20, 77, 82
  Bukhari v Bukhari 80
  Hayden v Family Education Trust 80–1
  Miller, Power v Turner 81, 84

Y

YouTube 12–13, 15, 19, 20–1
'YouTube Rewind' 119